Lasagna

Library of Congress Cataloging-in-Publication Data

Bishop, Jack.
Lasagna : classic and contemporary favorites / Jack Bishop.
p. cm.
Includes index.
ISBN 0-8092-3699-0 (pbk.)
1. Cookery (Pasta) 2. Cookery, Italian. I. Title.
TX809.M17B57 1994
641.8'22—dc20 93-44583
CIP

Cover design by Georgene Sainati
Cover photograph by Brian Leatart
Foodstyling by Norman Stewart
Prop styling by Kim Wong
Platter courtesy of Girasole

Featured on the cover: Lasagna with Broccoli, Carrots, and Red Bell Pepper

Published by Contemporary Books, Inc.
Two Prudential Plaza, Chicago, Illinois 60601-6790
Manufactured in the United States of America
International Standard Book Number: 0-8092-3699-0
10 9 8 7 6 5 4 3 2 1

To my grandmother
Katherine Pizzarello
for sharing the secrets of her lasagna

Contents

INTRODUCTION

A LASAGNA FOR EVERY OCCASION

Lasagna holds a very special place in my childhood memories. While other families were enjoying traditional goose, turkey, or ham at Christmas dinner, my Italian grandmother, Katherine Pizzarello, served lasagna. She spent days in the kitchen preparing noodles, simmering sauce, and stuffing the rolled round steak that would accompany the meal. The centerpiece of our holiday feast was what I called Nana's Classic Lasagna with Sausages and Braciole (see Index).

I suspect this elaborate meal is familiar to many Italian-Americans. I know my grandmother's siblings (all 11 of them) and their families consider this meal "Sunday dinner," to be eaten in midafternoon over the course of several hours. I remember as a child looking forward to those endless meals with countless relatives. Invariably I would overdo it and end up on the couch with my brother and sister, complaining of a bellyache. My grandmother's cooking was (and still is) so good it drove kids and even adults to excess.

Over the years my thoughts about food in general and lasagna in particular have changed. My childhood fondness for layered pasta dishes evolved while I lived in Florence about 10 years ago. A passion for traditional Italian food as prepared in the North, as opposed to the Italian-American classics made by my grandmother and inspired by the cooking of her mother's native Calabria, turned into a profession.

I learned to make pasta by hand, to recognize and use Italy's fine cheeses, and to experiment with foods not then readily available in the United States, like pancetta (Italian unsmoked bacon) and dried porcini (earthy mushrooms used in many sauces). With the increasing interest in Italian cuisine during the last decade, these ingredients as well as even more unusual items have become commonplace in American supermarkets and gourmet stores. It's now possible to cook with much the same ingredients that are available in markets in Milan or Rome.

But, of course, cooking in America can never be the same as the cooking in Florentine homes. For one thing, our lifestyle is very different from that of Italians. Perhaps most important are our national preoccupations with health and convenience. It's from this varied background that I began writing this book. Lasagna is comfort food from my childhood. It reflects the best in home cooking by using simple ingredients in creative but not forced ways. But lasagna can also work for modern cooks, like me, who are in need of dishes that can please so many different eaters.

My sister doesn't eat meat, friends are on low-fat diets, and the children in my family are notoriously picky eaters. Pasta is one of those rare dishes that appeal to just about everyone, and lasagna is no exception. As a bonus, unlike linguine or fettuccine, lasagna can be prepared in advance. The various components can be layered in the pan and then refrigerated for up to one day before baking.

So, if you're cooking for vegetarians, I've devoted a whole chapter (plus numerous recipes throughout the book) to meatless lasagna. Weekday cooks can turn to a chapter on quick recipes that use basic foodstuffs to create memorable meals in less than an hour. For special occasions or formal entertaining, I've assembled a chapter of sophisticated recipes that rely on slightly exotic or expensive ingredients like artichokes, endive, chicken livers, and veal.

In addition to the layered pasta recipes we call *lasagna*, I offer a number of "stacked" dishes using other hearty starches, namely polenta and potatoes. Cornmeal, called *polenta* by Italians, is actually quite traditional in lasagna-style dishes. My recipes using thin slices of potato may be a bit unconventional as lasagna, but their bold flavors will convert any skeptics.

A final caveat about cooking from this book. Feel free to make your own adaptations of recipes. Lasagna calls out for creativity, so use ingredients on hand. Most important, taste as you cook. Only you know how much salt or oregano your taste buds will enjoy. The recipes have been tested meticulously and will yield perfect results. However, you should always add a little more garlic or use a little less hot red pepper to suit a personal preference. This way my lasagna recipes will become your special favorites.

-1-

SECRETS FOR SUCCESS

The quality of any dish depends on the ingredients and the skill with which they are prepared. Lasagna is certainly no exception to this rule. To ensure success with the recipes in this book, follow these suggestions for buying and using essential ingredients like pasta, tomatoes, and cheese. Tips for cooking the noodles, assembling lasagna, and preparing ingredients in advance will help turn these basic foodstuffs into great meals.

Choosing Ingredients

Fresh Pasta: What is lasagna without good pasta? There is no question that the best lasagna is made with fresh noodles. Homemade noodles (five recipes are offered in Chapter 2) allow the cook to use a pasta that harmonizes with the sauce and cheeses in any given recipe. Throughout the book, recommendations are made for pastas particulary suited to a specific lasagna.

Luckily, it's no longer necessary to make your own fresh noodles. Even my grandmother relies on her supermarket for their excellent-quality sheets of fresh pasta. My local gourmet store sells everything from plain egg lasagna noodles to ones made from beets and carrots. Use these sheets as you would homemade pasta and ignore labels that advise against precooking. Although no-boil fresh noodles will work in lasagna dishes, I find that the results are better when noodles are cooked for 2 minutes and then refreshed in cold water. Instead of absorbing sauce as they cook, the noodles serve as a surface to which the sauce can cling.

Dried Pasta: Although fresh pasta is preferable, dried lasagna noodles also make excellent lasagna. In my experience Italian pastas, particularly the DeCecco brand, are superior to domestic products. DeCecco noodles are thinner and lighter than American noodles. In fact, while most domestic noodles come 18 or 20 to a pound, DeCecco has 28 sheets of pasta per pound. Therefore, recipes for lasagna with six layers call for 18 dried lasagna noodles (3 per layer) instead of specifying dry noodles by weight.

As for the dried no-boil noodles introduced several years ago, I had great difficulty working with them and do not recommend them in these recipes. Several brands were still tough when cooked, and all sucked liquid from the sauce. The resulting dish had chewy, not tender, noodles and very little sauce. To make these noodles work, you must add more liquid (either water or broth) to my recipes or use more liquid ingredients like tomato sauce. If you really want to skip pre-boiling the noodles, I suggest using very thin fresh noodles instead of dried no-boil noodles.

Cheeses: Almost every recipe in this book calls for at least one kind of cheese. Either whole-milk or part-skim mozzarella can be used in recipes. Whole-milk mozzarella is a bit creamier, but I tested every recipe with low-moisture part-skim cheese and was quite pleased with the results. Instead of buying cheese that has already been shredded, I prefer to shred the mozzarella (as well as other soft cheeses) myself in the food processor so that it doesn't dry out.

Due to its high moisture content, fresh mozzarella is a bit tricky to use in lasagna recipes. If you prefer to use mozzarella packed in water, be sure to dry the cheese on paper towels before shredding. Shredded cheese should then be placed in a strainer lined with more paper towels and drained for at least 30 minutes.

When it comes to buying Parmesan cheese, I cannot stress enough the importance of getting the real thing and grating it yourself. Pregrated cheese in bottles or even from a deli will not taste as good as that grated as it's needed, and Parmesan cheeses made in Argentina, Switzerland, or the United States will not have the same creamy, nutty flavor as real Italian Parmesan. If the cost of Reggiano seems too high, try grana padano, a less expensive type of Parmesan cheese but still quite worthy. In either case, always buy hunks of cheese with the rind attached and look for the words *Parmigiano-Reggiano* or *grana padano* stenciled on the rind.

When you get home, wrap pieces of Parmesan in plastic and place them in a zipper-lock bag. The cheese should stay fresh in the refrigerator for several weeks. As for grating, try the finest holes on a metal hand grater and ready cheese at the last moment and not in advance.

Tomatoes: The dismal state of the American supermarket tomato—often mealy, usually tasteless, and never ripe—has led many serious cooks to consider canned tomatoes their main source for making sauces. Although imported Italian plum tomatoes are an excellent product, I prefer crushed tomatoes from California for several reasons.

Imported tomatoes are often not nearly as fresh—some cans sit for months on ships—and can pick up a metallic flavor during their journey across the ocean. My favorite California brand, Redpack crushed tomatoes, is always sweet and never bitter or metallic-tasting. In addition, crushed tomatoes make quicker sauces, and since lasagna is often time-consuming I prefer to cut out work where possible.

When fresh tomatoes are called for in a recipe, use the oval plum variety rather than the round slicing types. Plum tomatoes, also known as Roma tomatoes, have fewer seeds and less juice, so they will be less watery in lasagna. Their sweet tomato flavor is also more dependable. Of course, if you have a favorite tomato sauce recipe, feel free to use it instead of the tomato sauces in Chapter 2.

A final thought about sauces: I avoid those from a jar for several reasons. First and foremost, I like to control the oil, salt, garlic, and seasonings that go into my sauce. Second, tomato sauce made with crushed tomatoes takes only 15 minutes to prepare and is vastly superior in flavor. Last, like my grandmother, I occasionally spend an hour or two making a traditional, slow-cooking tomato sauce on a quiet Sunday afternoon. I freeze extra sauce in small batches and defrost them as needed. It seems to me there are plenty of hassle-free alternatives to sauce from a jar.

Olive Oil: I have tried to keep oil to a minimum. When possible, sauté in a nonstick skillet and use a flavorful oil to get the most mileage from the fat that is added. Most of the recipes in this book call for olive oil. I usually select an inexpensive extra-virgin oil (my favorite is Colavita) for sauces. Reserve pricey extra-virgin oils for salad dressings or tossing on warm vegetables. If you prefer, a good pure olive oil can also be used in lasagna recipes, as can vegetable oils.

Béchamel Sauce: This creamy white sauce binds layers of lasagna together and is used in most recipes without tomato sauce and mozzarella. Nothing more than milk, flour, butter, and salt, this sauce is essential for both flavor and adhesion. Two versions—one traditional and one lower in fat—are given in Chapter 2. Either version can be used in recipes that call for béchamel. The traditional sauce is a bit creamier and thicker, although the lower-fat sauce is more than adequate. Béchamel takes only a few minutes to prepare but can be made several hours in advance and reheated when needed.

Most recipes call for slightly more béchamel than is actually used. It's better to discard a couple of tablespoons than to be caught short when assembling a lasagna. For a richer dish, drizzle excess béchamel (up to ¼ cup) around the edges of the pan so that it seeps down to the layers below.

Boiling Noodles

There are several important things to remember when precooking noodles for lasagna. Always boil noodles in an abundant quantity of water and stir frequently to prevent sticking. Although 1 gallon of water is usually sufficient to cook 1 pound of pasta, I recommend 5 quarts to ensure that large lasagna noodles do not stick together. Do not add oil to water—it will make noodles slick and difficult to retrieve—but do add salt for flavor.

Fresh noodles should be cooked four or five at a time for about 2 minutes. It's very hard to taste large noodles, so rely on this time guideline and remember that fresh noodles can easily be overcooked but are hard to undercook. Use a large slotted spoon to retrieve noodles and transfer them to a bowl of ice-cold water. After noodles have cooled (about 30 seconds), drain them and place on a clean kitchen towel to dry. Repeat the process with the remaining noodles.

Dried lasagna noodles can be cooked all at once. Cooking instructions for individual brands are a good guideline, but I usually shave off 1 minute just to be on the safe side. Again, it's quite hard to taste large dried noodles as they cook. If there are small scraps of broken pasta in the box, I usually add a few of them to the boiling water and retrieve them to get an idea of how the noodles are progressing. When dried lasagna noodles are just beginning to become al dente, drain them in a colander and then transfer them to a large bowl of ice-cold water. Drain the noodles again and place on a clean kitchen towel to dry.

Cooked noodles, both fresh and dried, can be covered with towels and set aside for about 1 hour before use.

Tricks for Assembling

Once the sauce has been made, the cheese grated, and the pasta boiled, you are ready to assemble the lasagna. Recipes in this book call for a lasagna pan (usually about 2 inches deep) that measures 13″ × 9″. A glass, metal, or ceramic pan with relatively sharp corners is easier to work with than a pan with round corners.

Vegetable oil sprays are the fastest and most convenient way to grease the bottom and sides of the pan, although butter may be used if desired. To prevent the bottom layer of pasta from sticking and drying out, several tablespoons of béchamel or tomato sauce (minus large chunks of vegetables or meat) are usually smeared across the bottom of the pan. Use the back of a large spoon or a plastic spatula to coat the pan with a thin film of sauce.

Constructing a good lasagna depends on even layers of pasta. Don't worry if dried pasta looks too small. The noodles swell when boiled and fit evenly into a 13″ × 9″ pan. Three noodles of most brands will fit into the pan, running lengthwise. However, DeCecco noodles are shorter and wider than the American noodles and should be layered across the width of the greased pan.

Fresh noodles will have to be cut to fit. Place the noodle in the pan and use a small sharp knife or scissors to trim it if necessary. Fresh noodles expand even more than dried ones when boiled, so don't worry if it looks as if you won't have enough to make six layers when rolling them out.

When spreading sauce, drizzling béchamel, or sprinkling cheese over layers of pasta, it is important to make sure that ingredients are divided evenly over the entire surface. Avoid large clumps and be sure to cut vegetables fairly small (or break apart clumps of meat when browning) so that they will fit snugly between layers of pasta. Recipes call for specific amounts of various ingredients per layer. However, these measurements are only guidelines. Sometimes sauces will cook down more or less than expected, and you don't want to be caught short when you get to the top. Before assembling the dish, read through the recipe so that you will know how much béchamel or cheese is needed for top layers.

Some noodles may break during boiling. Piece together broken noodles in middle layers and reserve whole noodles to build a strong base on the bottom and an attractive finish on the top. The top layer of pasta is often coated with just béchamel and/or cheese. Pieces of vegetables will dry out, so they are rarely put on top. For lasagna with just cheese on top, be sure to sprinkle the surface evenly. If coated with béchamel, use a plastic spatula or the back of a spoon to spread sauce over the whole top. Uncovered noodles will dry out or burn in the oven.

Do-Ahead Suggestions

Ingredients can be prepared and set aside at room temperature for an hour or two, or even better, the lasagna can be assembled and refrigerated or even frozen. (Assembled lasagna will become soggy at room temperature, so always chill it.) Tightly wrap an assembled lasagna in aluminum foil and refrigerate it for several hours or even overnight. To freeze an uncooked lasagna, wrap the pan tightly in plastic and then in foil. The lasagna will keep for a month and should be defrosted in the refrigerator for a day before being baked and served.

Baking Tips

When lasagna is overcooked, the vegetables and pasta become mushy and unappetizing. Therefore, brief baking (usually about 20 minutes) in a hot oven (usually about 400°F) is best. Place the filled pan in the middle of the oven and bake until the top turns golden brown in spots and the sauce is bubbling. Preassembled lasagna should be taken straight from the refrigerator but will need at least 5 extra minutes to heat through.

Cutting and Serving

It's a good idea to let hot lasagna settle before cutting. Depending on the water content of the sauce, 5 or 10 minutes should be enough time for the sauce, cheese, and pasta to solidify. Use a sharp knife and flexible spatula to get lasagna out of the pan. Small squares or rectangles, no larger than 3″ × 4″, are easiest to remove intact.

A Note About Serving Sizes

With the exception of the three dessert recipes, every lasagna in this book makes a complete meal when served with salad and bread. If your crowd is hungry or if you have skimped on hors d'oeuvres, plan on 6 adult servings from most recipes. When served as part of a large meal, standard-size lasagna will feed eight. Particularly hearty dishes with meat may even satisfy 10 people if there is plenty of other food on the table.

Leftover Lasagna

Leftover lasagna can be kept in the pan, wrapped in foil, and refrigerated for 2 days. To reheat, cut slices and wrap in foil or bake the whole pan covered with foil. Cold lasagna will take about 30 minutes to reheat in a 400°F oven. Pieces of lasagna can also be transferred to a plate and covered loosely with plastic and then microwaved for several minutes on HIGH to reheat. In either case, make sure the lasagna has been heated through by sticking the tip of a knife into the center for 2 or 3 seconds. It should come out quite hot.

-2-

THE BASICS

Master Recipe for Egg Pasta
Black Pepper Pasta
Herb Pasta
Spinach Pasta
Basil and Garlic Pasta
Master Recipe for Polenta
Quick Tomato Sauce
Fresh Tomato Sauce
Béchamel Sauce
Low-Fat Béchamel Sauce

Master Recipe for Egg Pasta

Making pasta from scratch is much easier than it sounds. The ingredients—nothing more than flour and eggs—could not be simpler. The dough may be kneaded by hand or in the food processor (see "Making Pasta Using a Food Processor"). I like the feel of kneading by hand, and everyone should try this method at least once. For convenience, however, nothing beats the food processor. As for rolling out the dough, I use an Atlas hand-cranked pasta machine. This device costs about $40 and most closely approximates hand-rolled dough. A rolling pin may be used, but it will be more difficult to get the pasta thin enough (see "Rolling by Hand"). To make more than six layers, increase proportions to 2⅔ cups flour and 4 eggs.

MAKES ENOUGH PASTA FOR 6 LAYERS IN A STANDARD 13″ × 9″ LASAGNA PAN

2 cups all-purpose flour
3 large eggs
5 quarts water
1 tablespoon salt

1. Place flour on a clean, dry work surface (a countertop or wood surface is best). With your hands, shape flour into a 6-inch ring with an empty well in the center. Crack eggs into this well and beat lightly with a fork. Slowly work in some of the flour from the inside of the ring. Continue incorporating flour from around the inside of the ring as the egg mixture becomes thicker.

2. Eventually the walls of the flour ring will collapse. Continue using a fork to incorporate flour into the sticky egg mass. Use your hands to knead dough into a solid ball for about 1 minute. Incorporate as much flour as necessary to keep dough from being very sticky.

3. At this point, set dough aside (it will still have chunks of unincorporated flour in it) and clean your hands and the work surface. Small bits of dried flour will cause lumps in the pasta and must be removed, so wash and thoroughly dry the work surface. Wash and dry your hands and dust them lightly with flour.

4. Return dough to work surface and continue kneading by hand. If small bits of hardened dough fall off, sweep them to the side of the surface or move dough

ball to a clean part of the surface. In any case, do not try to incorporate these pieces into the dough. Continue kneading until dough is quite smooth and not sticky. As my Florentine pasta teacher told me, "Pasta dough should be as smooth as a baby's behind." Kneading should take about 10 minutes.

5. Shape dough into a ball, wrap tightly in plastic, and set aside for at least 15 minutes to let dough relax. If tightly wrapped, the dough can be set aside at room temperature for several hours.

6. Set up a hand-cranked pasta machine and cover a large area with paper towels. Unwrap dough and knead for about 1 minute to incorporate the moisture that has formed on its surface.

7. Slice a ½-inch piece of dough (you should be able to get about six slices from the dough ball) and flatten it into a disk. (Rewrap remaining dough to prevent it from drying out as you work.) Run disk through widest setting on pasta machine. Bring ends of dough toward the middle and press down to seal. Run the open end through the first setting again. Repeat folding, sealing, and rolling once. Without folding, run pasta through first setting two times or until dough is smooth. (If dough is at all sticky, lightly dust it with flour.) Continue running dough through rollers, narrowing the setting each time until dough is quite thin and the outline of your hand is visible through the pasta (usually setting 6 on the Atlas machine). If at any time the dough breaks or holes form, roll pasta back into a ball, return machine to first setting, and begin the process again.

8. Set pasta sheet aside on paper towels. It will probably be quite long and should be sliced in half. Continue the process until all of the dough has been rolled into sheets.

9. Bring the water to a boil in a large stockpot. Add salt and four sheets of pasta when water is at a rolling boil. Cook pasta, stirring occasionally, until tender, about 2 minutes. Use a slotted spoon to retrieve lasagna noodles and transfer them to a bowl of cold water. Once noodles are refreshed, about 30 seconds, transfer them to a clean kitchen towel to dry. Repeat process, cooking about four noodles at a time. Use cooked noodles within 1 hour.

Do-Ahead Tips

If you would like to roll out the pasta in the morning, set it aside on paper towels to dry for several hours. Cook slightly dried fresh pasta an extra 30 seconds to 1 minute. To store fresh pasta for up to 1 week, place dried noodles (they should have the texture of fruit leather) in a plastic zipper-lock bag and refrigerate. Allow pasta to come to room temperature before boiling for 3 or 4 minutes.

⚘

Making Pasta Using a Food Processor

All of the pasta recipes can be made in a large food processor instead of by hand. Place the flour and any seasonings in a work bowl fitted with the metal blade and pulse several times to mix ingredients well. Add the eggs and process until dough forms a rough ball, about 30 seconds. If any small, pebblelike chunks of dough refuse to become part of the large mass, remove ball and small pieces of dough from machine and knead together until smooth, about 1 minute. Wrap dough in plastic and set aside to rest for 15 minutes. Roll and cook pasta as directed in steps 6–9 of the Master Recipe for Egg Pasta.

⚘

Rolling by Hand

In many Italian kitchens, pasta dough is rolled out into one gigantic thin sheet using a 3-foot-long rolling pin. This technique takes much practice. An easier but less authentic rolling method can be used instead. Follow the directions in the Master Recipe for Egg Pasta through step 6. Slice off ½-inch-thick pieces of dough and roll them into very thin sheets. A long French rolling pin without handles is best for the job, although an American-style pin with handles can also be used. The dough should be very thin, and the outline of your hand should be visible though the pasta.

Black Pepper Pasta

❧

Coarsely ground black pepper adds a sparkle to plain egg noodles. Use these noodles with simple sauces that need some dressing up. *See page 14 for instructions for preparing dough in the food processor.*

MAKES ENOUGH PASTA FOR 6 LAYERS IN A STANDARD 13″ × 9″ LASAGNA PAN

2 cups all-purpose flour
3 large eggs
1½ teaspoons freshly ground black pepper

1. Place flour on a clean, dry work surface (a countertop or wood surface is best). With your hands, shape flour into a 6-inch ring with an empty well in the center. Crack eggs into this well and add the pepper. Beat eggs and pepper lightly with a fork until well mixed. Slowly work in some of the flour from the inside of the ring. Continue incorporating flour from around the inside of the ring as the egg mixture becomes thicker.

2. Knead, roll, and cook the pasta as directed in steps 2–9 of the Master Recipe for Egg Pasta (see Index).

Best Lasagna for Black Pepper Pasta

Lasagna with Turkey Sausage, Green Peppers, and Onions
Lasagna with Spicy Cauliflower Sauce
Lasagna with Dried Mushrooms and Parmesan
Lasagna with Endive and Radicchio
Black Pepper Lasagna with Caramelized Onions and Pancetta
Louisiana Lasagna

Herb Pasta

❧

Since they are relatively mild in flavor, parsley and basil are the traditional choices for herb pasta. However, more assertive herbs like sage, thyme, oregano, marjoram, and cilantro may be used in dishes with tomato sauce or other strongly flavored ingredients. *See page 14 for instructions for preparing dough in the food processor.*

MAKES ENOUGH PASTA FOR 6 LAYERS IN A STANDARD 13″ × 9″ LASAGNA PAN

2 cups all-purpose flour
3 large eggs
2 tablespoons very finely minced fresh herbs

1. Place flour on a clean, dry work surface (a countertop or wood surface is best). With your hands, shape flour into a 6-inch ring with an empty well in the center. Crack eggs into this well and add herbs. Beat eggs and herbs lightly with a fork until well mixed. Slowly work in some of the flour from the inside of the ring. Continue incorporating flour from around the inside of the ring as the egg mixture becomes thicker.

2. Knead, roll, and cook the pasta as directed in steps 2–9 of the Master Recipe for Egg Pasta (see Index).

Best Lasagna for Herb Pasta

Lasagna with Tricolor Bell Peppers
Lasagna with Sun-Dried Tomato Pesto
Lasagna with Spicy Broccoli Sauce
Sicilian-Style Lasagna with Cauliflower and Green Olives
Lasagna Primavera
Lasagna with Broccoli, Carrots, and Red Bell Pepper
Lasagna with Spring Greens and Wild Mushrooms
Lasagna with Zucchini and Shiitake Mushrooms
Lasagna with Creamy Spinach and Gorgonzola
Artichoke Lasagna with Tomato-Garlic Sauce
Lasagna with Baked Squash, Prosciutto, and Pine Nuts
Spring Lasagna with Leeks and Artichokes
Parsley Lasagna with Scallops and Bread Crumbs
Lasagna with Shrimp and Sun-Dried Tomato Sauce

Spinach Pasta

Because of the liquid in the spinach, this is probably the most difficult pasta for beginners to make successfully. Squeeze out as much water as possible from the cooked greens, or the dough will be very sticky. If you find that the dough is gummy, knead in more flour until it is smooth. See page 14 for instructions for preparing dough in the food processor.

MAKES ENOUGH PASTA FOR 6 LAYERS IN A STANDARD 13″ × 9″ LASAGNA PAN

1 cup water
½ 10-ounce package frozen chopped spinach, thawed
2½ cups all-purpose flour
3 large eggs

1. Bring water to a boil in a small pan. Add spinach and cook until tender, about three minutes. Drain and refresh spinach under cold running water. Use your hands to press out all the liquid from the spinach.

2. Transfer spinach to a cutting board and chop fine. Press your hands against spinach and tilt the cutting board over a sink to squeeze out any remaining liquid. There should be about ⅓ cup very finely chopped, completely dry spinach.

3. Place flour on a clean, dry work surface (a countertop or wood surface is best). With your hands, shape flour into a 6-inch ring with an empty well in the center. Crack eggs into this well and add spinach. Beat eggs and spinach lightly with a fork until well mixed. Slowly work in some of the flour from the inside of the ring. Continue incorporating flour from around the inside of the ring as the egg mixture becomes thicker.

4. Knead, roll, and cook the pasta as directed in steps 2–9 of the Master Recipe for Egg Pasta (see Index).

Cook's Note: Frozen spinach is easier to work with than fresh, and this is one of those rare occasions when nothing is sacrificed by using the frozen product. If you have fresh spinach on hand, boil about ½ pound in abundant water until tender, about 2 minutes, and follow the same directions for frozen spinach.

Best Lasagna for Spinach Pasta

Lasagna with Quick Meat Sauce and Ricotta Salata
Lasagna with Broccoli, Sausage, and Tomatoes
Lasagna with Bolognese Meat Sauce
Lasagna Cacciatore
Lasagna with Sausage and Ricotta
Lasagna "Paglia e Fieno"
Nana's Lasagna with Tiny Meatballs
Lasagna with Chicken, Prosciutto, and Spinach
Lasagna with Snow Peas, Mushrooms, and Tomatoes
Lasagna with Braised Cannellini Beans
Elegant Pesto Lasagna
Chicken Liver Lasagna with Balsamic Vinegar and Tomatoes
Greek Lasagna

Basil and Garlic Pasta

This recipe captures the flavor of pesto in a noodle. If you're making this pasta in a food processor (see page 14 for more details), mince the garlic and basil first and then add the flour. Whether the dough is made by hand or in the machine, it is essential that the basil leaves be very dry.

MAKES ENOUGH PASTA FOR 6 LAYERS IN A STANDARD 13″ × 9″ LASAGNA PAN

2 cups all-purpose flour
3 large eggs
½ cup tightly packed fresh basil leaves, minced fine
2 cloves garlic, minced fine

1. Place flour on a clean, dry work surface (a countertop or wood surface is best). With your hands, shape the flour into a 6-inch ring with an empty well in the center. Crack eggs into this well and add basil and garlic. Beat eggs, basil, and garlic lightly with a fork until well mixed. Slowly work in some of the flour from the inside of the ring. Continue incorporating flour from around the inside of the ring as the egg mixture becomes thicker.

2. Knead, roll, and cook the pasta as directed in steps 2–9 of the Master Recipe for Egg Pasta (see Index).

Best Lasagna for Basil and Garlic Pasta

Lasagna with Fresh Mozzarella, Tomatoes, and Basil
Lasagna with Asparagus, Basil, and Parmesan
Lasagna with Eggplant, Basil, and Tomatoes
Elegant Pesto Lasagna
Lasagna with Shrimp and Sun-Dried Tomato Sauce

Master Recipe for Polenta

Polenta is coarse-grained yellow cornmeal that is commonly served instead of pasta in northern Italy. Soft polenta may be eaten warm with a hearty tomato sauce. Slightly thicker polenta is usually cooled and then cut into squares that can be used as pasta sheets in lasagna or grilled and served with roasted meats. Instant polenta (the cornmeal has been precooked and then dried) is ready to use in only a few minutes and works just as well as the slow-cooking version in lasagna recipes. Look for Fattorie & Pandea instant polenta or other imported brands in better supermarkets and gourmet stores. Regular polenta can be used—just follow the package directions for cooking time.

MAKES ENOUGH POLENTA FOR 2 LAYERS IN A STANDARD 13″ × 9″ LASAGNA PAN

7 cups water
2 teaspoons salt
2 cups instant polenta

1. Bring water to a boil in a deep saucepan. Add salt and then polenta in a steady stream, stirring constantly with a wooden spoon as you pour. Reduce heat to medium-low and continue stirring as polenta thickens and bubbles. (Take care that polenta does not splatter onto your hands or face.) Cook, stirring constantly, until polenta is very thick, about 2 minutes.

2. Remove pan from heat and pour polenta onto two greased 13″ × 9″ cookie sheets. Cool for 15 minutes and cut polenta for use in recipes.

Quick Tomato Sauce

This simple sauce is used in numerous recipes throughout the book. Stronger herbs (such as oregano, thyme, and marjoram) may be substituted for the parsley or basil, but they can overwhelm delicate ingredients. Taste the sauce before adding salt. Some canned tomatoes are much saltier than others and may require very little extra seasoning.

MAKES ABOUT 3 CUPS

3 tablespoons olive oil
2 cloves garlic, minced fine
1 28-ounce can crushed tomatoes
2 tablespoons minced fresh parsley **or** ***basil leaves***
½ teaspoon salt or to taste
Several grindings of fresh black pepper

1. Heat oil in a medium-size saucepan. Add garlic and sauté over medium heat until pale yellow in color, about 1 minute.

2. Add tomatoes, herbs, salt, and pepper and bring sauce to a boil. Lower heat and simmer gently until sauce thickens slightly, about 10 minutes. Adjust salt and pepper as needed.

Hot Sauce Variation: Both this sauce and the Fresh Tomato Sauce that follows can be made spicy. Simply add ½ teaspoon hot red pepper flakes (more for a very hot sauce) along with garlic and proceed, omitting black pepper from Quick Tomato Sauce.

Fresh Tomato Sauce

This sauce captures the flavors of summer—ripe tomatoes, basil, garlic, and olive oil—all year-round. Oval-shaped plum tomatoes are better for sauce making than their round cousins since they are less juicy and rarely mealy.

MAKES ABOUT 3 CUPS

⅓ cup olive oil
1 tablespoon finely minced garlic
3 pounds very ripe plum tomatoes, peeled, seeded, and chopped (see "Peeling and Seeding Tomatoes")
3 tablespoons chopped fresh basil leaves
½ teaspoon salt

1. Heat oil in a medium-size saucepan. Add garlic and cook until pale yellow in color, about 1 minute.

2. Add tomatoes, basil, and salt and simmer gently over medium heat until tomatoes soften and mixture becomes a chunky sauce, about 30 minutes. Sauce may be used as is or pureed until smooth in a food mill or with a hand-held blender.

Peeling and Seeding Tomatoes

Tomato peels can disturb an otherwise smooth sauce, and the seeds can make a sauce too watery. Therefore, both are removed before fresh tomatoes are used. To peel tomatoes, bring a pot of water to a boil. Add tomatoes and turn several times with a large slotted spoon. Cook for about 30 seconds. Remove tomatoes with the spoon and cool. Peel off the skins with your fingers. To seed tomatoes, simply slice in half lengthwise and squeeze out the seeds. If necessary, use your fingers to remove seeds. Dice tomato pulp and use in sauces.

Béchamel Sauce

⚘

This simple white sauce, known as salsa besciamèlla in Italy, adds creaminess to many lasagna recipes. Nothing more than butter, flour, milk, and salt, it also serves as a thickener that binds the various layers of pasta and sauce together. The yield will vary, depending on the thickness of the sauce and cooking time. (The longer béchamel cooks, the thicker it becomes and the lower the yield.) I suggest preparing a full recipe and measuring out exactly the quantity specified in the ingredient list for individual lasagna recipes. Extra béchamel (up to ¼ cup) can be drizzled on top or around the edges for greater richness. Remember it's better to prepare a few tablespoons too much than too little.

MAKES ABOUT 2 CUPS

2 cups milk
4 tablespoons unsalted butter
3½ tablespoons all-purpose flour
¼ teaspoon salt

1. Gently heat milk in a small pan so that it is warm but not scalded.

2. Meanwhile, heat butter in a medium-size saucepan. When butter is foamy, whisk in flour until smooth. Stir and cook for 2 minutes over medium heat. Do not let flour brown.

3. Add several tablespoons of the hot milk, whisking constantly. When milk is thoroughly blended into butter and flour mixture, add several more tablespoons. Repeat until all the milk has been added and the sauce is smooth. If at any time the sauce separates or lumps form, whisk vigorously until smooth.

4. Add salt and cook sauce over medium heat for several minutes or until it thickens slightly and has the texture of heavy cream. Do not let it bubble. Remove pan from heat and use sauce immediately, or pour it into a glass measuring cup and cover with plastic wrap, placing plastic directly on the surface to keep a skin from forming. Keep at room temperature for up to 2 hours or refrigerate overnight. Reheat if chilled and whisk before using.

Low-Fat Béchamel Sauce

This lighter version of béchamel contains less than half the fat of the regular recipe and relies on heart-healthy olive oil instead of butter. It will be a bit thinner than the traditional sauce and slightly yellow because of the olive oil, but it can be used in any lasagna recipe. Note that the technique is somewhat different and does require a little extra time.

MAKES ABOUT 2 CUPS

2¼ cups low-fat milk
2½ tablespoons olive oil
2½ tablespoons all-purpose flour
¼ teaspoon salt

1. Gently heat milk in a small pan so that it is warm but not scalded.

2. Meanwhile, heat olive oil in a medium-size nonstick saucepan. Whisk in flour, stir, and cook over medium heat for 2 minutes. Do not let flour brown.

3. Whisk in all the milk at once and continue whisking to break up any lumps. Bring mixture to a boil and reduce heat so that sauce is simmering gently. Stir frequently as sauce thickens, making sure it does not stick to the bottom of the pan.

4. After about 10 minutes, the sauce should have the consistency of light cream. Remove pan from heat; stir in salt, and pour sauce through a fine-mesh strainer or briefly whip it in a blender if any lumps remain. Use sauce immediately or pour it into a glass measuring cup and cover with plastic wrap, placing plastic directly on the surface to keep a skin from forming. Keep at room temperature for up to 2 hours or refrigerate overnight. Reheat if chilled and whisk before using.

-3-

Quick Fixes

Lasagna with Tricolor Bell Peppers
Lasagna with Sun-Dried Tomato Pesto
Lasagna with Turkey Sausage, Green Peppers, and Onions
Lasagna with Fresh Mozzarella, Tomatoes, and Basil
Lasagna with Quick Meat Sauce and Ricotta Salata
Lasagna with Spicy Broccoli Sauce
Polenta Lasagna with Sausage, Spinach, and Tomatoes
Polenta Lasagna with Arugula and Smoked Mozzarella

Lasagna with Tricolor Bell Peppers

This colorful and quick dish is enlivened by green, red, and yellow bell peppers and a healthy dose of garlic. Fresh herbs and mozzarella cheese round out the flavors.

SERVES 6–8

¼ cup olive oil
4 cloves garlic, minced
2 large (about 1 pound) green bell peppers, cut into ¼-inch-thick strips
2 large (about 1 pound) red bell peppers, cut into ¼-inch-thick strips
2 large (about 1 pound) yellow bell peppers, cut into ¼-inch-thick strips
1 tablespoon minced fresh oregano leaves
2 tablespoons minced fresh parsley leaves
1 teaspoon salt
½ teaspoon freshly ground black pepper
1 recipe Egg Pasta **or** ***Herb Pasta (see Index)*** **or** ***18 dried lasagna noodles***
1 pound mozzarella cheese, shredded

1. Heat oil in a large skillet. Add garlic and sauté over medium heat until lightly colored, 1 to 2 minutes. Add pepper strips and cook, stirring occasionally, until slightly softened but not mushy, about 5 minutes. Stir in herbs, salt, and pepper and set aside.

2. Cook and drain pasta. Preheat oven to 400°F.

3. Grease a 13″ × 9″ lasagna pan. Line bottom with a layer of pasta, making sure noodles touch but do not overlap. Spread 1 cup peppers and any liquid that has accumulated in the pan over pasta and sprinkle with ⅔ cup cheese. Repeat layering of pasta, peppers, and cheese four more times. For the sixth layer, spread

remaining 1 cup peppers and their juices over pasta and sprinkle with remaining 1 cup cheese.

4. Bake lasagna until cheese turns golden brown in spots, about 20 minutes. Remove pan from oven, let lasagna settle for 5 minutes, and serve.

A Colorful Vegetable

Many cooks are surprised to learn that green, red, yellow, orange, and purple bell peppers all come from the same plant. Green peppers are picked before they are ripe and are usually a bit bitter. As peppers mature on the vine, they become noticeably sweeter and turn either red, yellow, orange, or purplish-black in color, depending on the species. Fully ripe peppers are more perishable than green ones and therefore are usually more expensive in grocery stores. When using just one kind of pepper, I usually opt for the sweeter red or yellow variety. In recipes with several kinds of peppers, I include green ones for color and flavor contrast.

Lasagna with Sun-Dried Tomato Pesto

The sauce for this lasagna does not need to be cooked. Simply puree rehydrated sun-dried tomatoes with garlic, olive oil, and crushed tomatoes and then stir in two cheeses and fresh basil.

SERVES 6–8

¼ pound sun-dried tomatoes (see "Sun-Dried Tomatoes")
2 tablespoons olive oil
3 cloves garlic
2 cups canned crushed tomatoes
1 teaspoon salt
½ teaspoon freshly ground black pepper
2 cups ricotta cheese
1 cup freshly grated Parmesan cheese
⅓ cup tightly packed basil leaves, cut into strips
1 recipe Egg Pasta* or *Herb Pasta (see Index)* or *18 dried lasagna noodles

1. Place sun-dried tomatoes in a bowl, cover with boiling water, and soak for 15 minutes. Drain tomatoes and reserve ⅓ cup soaking liquid.

2. Puree rehydrated tomatoes in a food processor or blender along with olive oil, garlic, crushed tomatoes, salt, pepper, and reserved soaking liquid until smooth.

3. Combine ricotta, ½ cup Parmesan cheese, and basil in a large bowl. Stir in sun-dried tomato pesto and mix well.

4. Cook and drain pasta. Preheat oven to 375°F.

5. Grease a 13″ × 9″ lasagna pan. Line bottom with a layer of pasta, making sure noodles touch but do not overlap. Spread 1 cup pesto over pasta. Repeat to make six layers of pasta covered with sauce. Sprinkle remaining ½ cup Parmesan over top layer.

6. Bake lasagna until cheese turns golden brown in spots and sauce is bubbling, about 20 minutes. Remove pan from oven, let lasagna settle for 5 minutes, and serve.

Sun-Dried Tomatoes

I buy dried tomatoes in bulk and then reconstitute only as many as I need at one time. This way I control the oil and seasonings added to my tomatoes. If you prefer, sun-dried tomatoes packed in extra-virgin olive oil can be used in this recipe. Lift the tomatoes from the oil and then puree with the other ingredients, adding 2 tablespoons olive oil to replace the soaking liquid.

Lasagna with Turkey Sausage, Green Peppers, and Onions

This surprisingly quick recipe combines sausage, peppers, and onions in a light, flavorful tomato sauce. Best of all, it is quite lean but sacrifices nothing in flavor.

SERVES 6–8

2 tablespoons olive oil
2 onions, peeled and chopped coarse
1 pound low-fat turkey sausage
2 green bell peppers, chopped
1 recipe Quick Tomato Sauce (see Index)
Salt and freshly ground black pepper to taste
1 recipe Egg Pasta **or** ***Black Pepper Pasta (see Index)*** **or** ***18 dried lasagna noodles***
1 pound mozzarella cheese, shredded

1. Heat oil in a large nonstick skillet. Add onions and cook over medium heat until very soft and translucent, about 10 minutes. Squeeze sausage from casings directly into the skillet and use a fork to crumble meat. When sausage has browned, about 5 minutes, add green peppers. Cook, stirring occasionally, until peppers have softened slightly but are not mushy, about 5 minutes more. Stir in tomato sauce and season with salt and pepper. Simmer for 5 minutes to blend flavors and set aside.

2. Cook and drain pasta. Preheat oven to 400°F.

3. Grease a 13″ × 9″ lasagna pan. Smear several tablespoons of sauce (without large chunks of vegetables or meat) across bottom. Line bottom with a layer of pasta, making sure noodles touch but do not overlap. Spread about 1 cup sauce

over pasta and sprinkle with ⅔ cup cheese. Repeat layering of pasta, sauce, and cheese four more times. For the sixth layer, cover pasta with remaining ½ cup sauce and sprinkle generously with remaining 1 cup cheese.

4. Bake lasagna until cheese turns golden brown in spots and sauce is bubbling, about 20 minutes. Remove pan from oven, let lasagna settle for 5 minutes, and serve.

Cook's Note: To save even more calories, omit the olive oil and coat the skillet with a thin film of vegetable spray before sautéing the onions.

Lasagna with Fresh Mozzarella, Tomatoes, and Basil

This summery lasagna does not require any precooking of ingredients and is especially quick to prepare. Be sure to follow the procedures outlined for removing excess moisture from the fresh mozzarella and tomatoes.

SERVES 6

1 pound fresh mozzarella cheese packed in water
2½ pounds very ripe plum tomatoes
¾ cup chopped fresh basil leaves
2 cloves garlic, minced fine
1 cup freshly grated Parmesan cheese
½ cup unseasoned bread crumbs, toasted
2 tablespoons olive oil
1 teaspoon salt
½ teaspoon freshly ground black pepper
1 recipe Egg Pasta* or *Basil and Garlic Pasta (see Index)* or *18 dried lasagna noodles

1. Remove excess moisture from mozzarella by drying exterior with paper towels. Shred mozzarella and place in a colander lined with paper towels to absorb more moisture. Set aside.

2. Trim stem end from each tomato and cut in half lengthwise. Squeeze out seeds and liquid (if necessary, use your fingers to scoop out seeds) and discard. Chop tomato pulp into small cubes and set aside in a large bowl.

3. Toss basil, garlic, Parmesan, bread crumbs, olive oil, salt, and pepper with tomatoes. Stir in all but 1 cup shredded mozzarella. Mix well and taste for salt.

4. Cook and drain pasta. Preheat oven to 400°F.

5. Grease a 13″ × 9″ lasagna pan. Line bottom with a layer of pasta, making sure noodles touch but do not overlap. Spread 1½ cups tomato mixture evenly over pasta. Repeat layering of pasta and tomato mixture four more times. For the sixth layer, cover pasta with reserved 1 cup shredded mozzarella.

6. Bake lasagna until cheese turns golden brown in spots, about 15 minutes. Remove pan from oven, let lasagna settle for 10 minutes, and serve.

Cook's Note: If the lasagna appears at all watery, lift cut pieces from the pan with a slotted spatula and let excess liquid drip back into the pan.

Lasagna with Quick Meat Sauce and Ricotta Salata

❧

Ricotta salata is a dry, slightly crumbly cheese that combines the sharpness of aged Parmesan with the creaminess of fresh ricotta. This wonderful cheese has just recently been imported to America in large quantities and is now available in better supermarkets and cheese shops. If you cannot locate it, substitute equal portions of regular ricotta and either Pecorino Romano (a pungent sheep's milk cheese) or Parmesan.

SERVES 6–8

2 tablespoons olive oil
1 tablespoon finely minced garlic
½ teaspoon hot red pepper flakes
1 pound ground beef
1 28-ounce can crushed tomatoes
2 teaspoons minced fresh oregano leaves **or** ***½ teaspoon dried***
½ teaspoon salt or less, depending on saltiness of cheese
1 recipe Egg Pasta **or** ***Spinach Pasta (see Index)*** **or** ***18 dried lasagna noodles***
⅔ pound ricotta salata, shredded

1. Heat oil in a large saucepan. Add garlic and red pepper flakes and sauté over medium heat until garlic is golden, about 2 minutes. Add meat and crumble with a fork. Cook until the meat loses its red color, about 3 minutes. Add tomatoes, oregano, and salt and simmer gently until sauce thickens slightly, about 10 minutes.

2. Cook and drain pasta. Preheat oven to 425°F.

3. Grease a 13″ × 9″ lasagna pan. Line bottom with a layer of pasta, making sure noodles touch but do not overlap. Spread about ⅔ cup meat sauce over pasta and sprinkle with ⅓ cup cheese. Repeat to make a total of six layers.

4. Cover pan with aluminum foil and bake for 15 minutes. Remove foil and bake until sauce is bubbling, about 5 minutes more. Remove pan from oven, let lasagna settle for 5 minutes, and serve.

Lasagna with Spicy Broccoli Sauce

Broccoli is sparked by hot red pepper flakes, plenty of garlic, minced anchovies, and a squirt of lemon juice in this simple but satisfying lasagna.

SERVES 6–8

2 small heads (about 2½ pounds) broccoli
Salt to taste
⅓ cup olive oil
2 tablespoons finely minced garlic
1 teaspoon hot red pepper flakes
4 flat anchovy fillets, minced fine
¼ cup chopped pitted black olives
3 tablespoons fresh lemon juice
2 cups canned crushed tomatoes
1 recipe Egg Pasta* or *Herb Pasta (see Index)* or *18 lasagna noodles
1 pound mozzarella cheese, shredded

1. Trim and discard all but top inch or so from broccoli stalks. Remove tough skin from remaining stalks with a vegetable peeler and separate peeled stalks from the florets. Chop stalks into ¼-inch pieces and finely chop the florets. You should have about 6 cups chopped broccoli.

2. Bring several quarts of water to boil in a large pot. Add salt and chopped broccoli. Boil for 2 minutes, drain, and reserve.

3. Heat olive oil in a large saucepan. Add garlic, hot red pepper flakes, and anchovies and sauté over medium heat for 2 minutes. Stir in olives, lemon juice, and tomatoes and simmer for 5 minutes. Add boiled broccoli, mix well, and taste for salt. Set aside.

4. Cook and drain pasta. Preheat oven to 400°F.

5. Grease a 13″ × 9″ lasagna pan. Smear several tablespoons of tomato sauce (without large chunks of broccoli or olives) across bottom. Line bottom with a layer of pasta, making sure noodles touch but do not overlap. Spread 1 cup broccoli mixture over pasta and sprinkle with ⅔ cup cheese. Repeat layering of pasta, broccoli, and cheese four more times. For the sixth layer, spread remaining 1 cup broccoli over pasta and cover with remaining 1 cup cheese.

6. Bake lasagna until cheese turns golden brown in spots, about 20 minutes. Remove pan from oven, let lasagna settle for 5 minutes, and serve.

Cook's Note: I prefer the rich taste of oil-cured olives in this dish, but pitted black olives packed in brine can be used with good results.

Polenta Lasagna with Sausage, Spinach, and Tomatoes

Slices of polenta can be layered with sauce and assembled in serving bowls for a quick "lasagna." In this recipe, which takes about 30 minutes to prepare, a hearty tomato sauce studded with chunks of Italian sausage and spinach separates two squares of broiled or grilled polenta. Use hot sausage for a sauce with more punch.

SERVES 4

½ recipe Polenta (see Index)
1 tablespoon olive oil
1 onion, chopped
6 ounces sweet Italian sausage
⅓ pound spinach leaves **or** ***½ 10-ounce package frozen chopped spinach***
2 cups canned crushed tomatoes
½ teaspoon salt
¼ teaspoon freshly ground black pepper
½ cup freshly grated Parmesan cheese

1. Spread polenta evenly onto a greased 13″ × 9″ baking sheet.

2. Heat oil in a large skillet. Add onion and sauté over medium heat until translucent, about 5 minutes. Squeeze sausage from casings directly into pan. Break pieces apart with a wooden spoon or fork and fry until sausage loses its red color, about 4 minutes.

3. Wash fresh spinach (but do not dry it completely) and chop coarse. Add spinach along with any water clinging to its leaves to the skillet. Cook, stirring often, until spinach is wilted, about 3 minutes. If you're using frozen spinach, boil it until just tender and drain it well, add it to the skillet after sausage is cooked, and heat through for a minute or so. Add tomatoes, salt, and pepper and simmer gently over low heat until sauce thickens slightly, about 10 minutes.

4. While sauce is simmering, preheat broiler or light a grill. Place cookie sheet with polenta under broiler about 1 inch from heat, and cook until polenta is crisp and starting to turn golden brown, about 5 minutes. Remove pan from oven and cut polenta into eight squares. Or cut polenta into eight squares and grill several inches above heat source until golden brown on both sides, about 10 minutes altogether. Place one square on each of four serving plates. Ladle one-quarter of sauce over each portion and sprinkle with 2 tablespoons cheese. Top with remaining polenta squares and serve immediately.

Polenta Lasagna with Arugula and Smoked Mozzarella

❧

Usher in spring with this dish that combines bitter arugula greens with smoked mozzarella and tomatoes.

SERVES 4

½ recipe Polenta (see Index)
1 recipe Quick Tomato Sauce (see Index)
1 large bunch (about ¼ pound) arugula, chopped
½ pound smoked mozzarella cheese, shredded

1. Spread polenta evenly onto a greased 13″ × 9″ baking sheet.

2. Prepare Quick Tomato Sauce and preheat broiler or light a grill while it is simmering.

3. Place cookie sheet with polenta under broiler, about 1 inch from heat, and cook until polenta is crisp and starting to turn golden brown, about 5 minutes. Remove pan from oven and cut polenta into eight squares. Or cut polenta into eight squares and grill several inches above heat source until golden brown on both sides, about 10 minutes altogether.

4. Stir arugula into tomato sauce and cook until wilted, about 30 seconds.

5. Place one polenta square in each of four deep pasta bowls. Spread several tablespoons tomato sauce over each square and top each with a little cheese. Cover sauce with remaining polenta squares. Spread several tablespoons sauce over top of each portion and sprinkle with cheese. Serve immediately.

-4-

CLASSIC COMBINATIONS

Lasagna with Broccoli, Sausage, and Tomatoes
Spinach Lasagna with Bolognese Meat Sauce
Lasagna Cacciatore
Lasagna with Sausage and Ricotta
Lasagna "Paglia e Fieno"
Nana's Classic Lasagna with Sausages and Braciole
Nana's Lasagna with Tiny Meatballs
Sicilian-Style Lasagna with Cauliflower and Green Olives
Lasagna with Chicken, Prosciutto, and Spinach
Hearty Potato Lasagna with Kale and Chorizo
Potato Lasagna with Spinach, Mushrooms, and Gruyère
Polenta Lasagna with Chianti Meat Sauce

Lasagna with Broccoli, Sausage, and Tomatoes

This hearty tomato sauce is brimming with sausage and tender broccoli. Make sure the broccoli pieces are small enough to fit between layers of pasta and take care not to overcook them. Immediately rinsing the drained broccoli under cold water helps stop the cooking process.

SERVES 8

2 small heads (about 2½ pounds) broccoli
Salt to taste
2 tablespoons olive oil
2 onions, chopped
¾ pound sweet Italian sausage
1 28-ounce can crushed tomatoes
½ teaspoon dried oregano
½ teaspoon freshly ground black pepper
1 recipe Egg Pasta* or *Spinach Pasta (see Index)* or *18 dried lasagna noodles
1 pound mozzarella cheese, shredded

1. Trim and discard broccoli stalks. Cut florets into 1-inch pieces. You should have about 6 cups.

2. Bring a large pot of lightly salted water to a boil. Add broccoli and cook until crisp-tender, about 2 minutes. Drain broccoli, refresh under cold running water, and drain again. Chop broccoli very fine and set aside.

3. Heat oil in a large saucepan. Add onion and sauté over medium heat until translucent, about 5 minutes. Squeeze sausage from casings directly into saucepan. Use a fork or heavy spoon to break sausage into very small pieces. Cook until sausage is browned, about 5 minutes.

4. Stir in tomatoes, oregano, salt to taste (use salt sparingly if sausage is salty), and pepper. Bring sauce to a boil, reduce heat, and simmer gently for 10 minutes. Stir in chopped broccoli and set aside.

5. Cook and drain pasta. Preheat oven to 400°F.

6. Grease a 13″ × 9″ lasagna pan. Smear several tablespoons of tomato sauce (without large chunks of meat or vegetables) across bottom. Line bottom with a layer of pasta, making sure noodles touch but do not overlap. Spread 1 cup sauce over noodles and sprinkle with ⅔ cup cheese. Repeat layering of pasta, sauce, and cheese four more times. For the sixth layer, cover noodles with remaining 1 cup cheese.

7. Bake lasagna until cheese turns golden brown in spots and sauce is bubbling, about 20 minutes. Remove pan from oven, let lasagna settle for 5 minutes, and serve.

Spinach Lasagna with Bolognese Meat Sauce

Many experts consider the city of Bologna to be the gastronomic capital of Italy. Even those who are swayed by the cooking of Rome, Florence, or Venice agree that this meat sauce is among Italy's finest. The secret is very slow cooking in a heavy cast-iron or copper pan. As for the pasta, only fresh will do justice to the sauce.

SERVES 6

2 tablespoons olive oil
1 tablespoon unsalted butter
½ small onion, chopped
1 small carrot, chopped
1 small rib celery, chopped
1 pound ground round
½ cup dry white wine
½ cup milk
3 cups canned crushed tomatoes
1 teaspoon salt or more to taste
1 recipe Spinach Pasta (see Index)
1½ cups Béchamel Sauce (see Index)
1 cup freshly grated Parmesan cheese

1. Heat oil and butter in a large, very heavy copper or cast-iron saucepan. Add onion and sauté over medium heat until slightly wilted, about 4 minutes. Add carrot and celery and continue cooking until vegetables soften, about 5 minutes more.

2. Add meat and use a fork or the back of a spoon to break it into small pieces. As soon as the meat loses its red color, add wine and simmer until the aroma of the wine fades, about 4 minutes. Add milk and simmer until liquid in pan is clear again, about 4 minutes.

3. Add tomatoes and 1 teaspoon salt and reduce heat to low. Allow sauce to simmer very gently (sauce can be ruined by high heat but not by low heat), stirring occasionally, for 2½ to 3 hours. Finished sauce will be thick with no excess liquid floating on top. Taste for salt and set aside.

4. Cook and drain pasta. Preheat oven to 400°F.

5. Grease a 13″ × 9″ lasagna pan. Smear 3 tablespoons béchamel across bottom. Line bottom with a layer of pasta, making sure noodles touch but do not overlap. Smear ⅔ cup meat sauce over noodles and drizzle with 3 tablespoons béchamel. Sprinkle with 2 tablespoons cheese. Repeat layering of pasta, meat sauce, béchamel, and cheese four more times. For the sixth layer, coat noodles with 6 tablespoons béchamel and sprinkle with remaining 6 tablespoons cheese.

6. Bake lasagna until top turns golden brown in spots and sauce is bubbling, about 20 minutes. Remove pan from oven, let lasagna settle for 5 minutes, and serve.

Cook's Note: Since this meat sauce takes so long to cook (preparation time is actually less than 30 minutes), consider making a double recipe. Leftover sauce can be frozen and is perfect with fettuccine, ravioli, gnocchi, or tortellini.

Lasagna Cacciatore

The word cacciatore *is Italian for "hunter" and when used in recipes refers to a tomato-based sauce that is hearty enough to satisfy after a day in the woods. In this version sautéed skinless chicken breasts are paired with a vegetable-packed tomato sauce to make a hearty and healthy classic. Once the chicken is browned, set it aside and build the sauce in the same pan to save on cleanup.*

SERVES 6–8

¼ cup olive oil
¾ pound skinless, boneless chicken breasts, fat trimmed
Salt and freshly ground black pepper to taste
2 onions, sliced thin
4 cloves garlic, minced
10 ounces fresh white mushrooms, trimmed and sliced thin
1 large red bell pepper, cut into ½-inch dice
1 28-ounce can crushed tomatoes
¼ cup minced fresh parsley leaves
1 recipe Egg Pasta* or *Spinach Pasta (see Index)* or *18 dried lasagna noodles
1 pound mozzarella cheese, shredded

1. Heat 2 tablespoons of the olive oil in a large saucepan. Add chicken, sprinkle generously with salt and pepper, and cook over medium heat until browned, about 6 minutes. Turn chicken, sprinkle again with salt and pepper, and cook until fully cooked, about 5 minutes more. Remove chicken from pan. When cool, shred chicken and set aside.

2. Add remaining 2 tablespoons olive oil to pan along with onions. Sauté until onions are wilted and beginning to caramelize, about 10 minutes. Stir in garlic and mushrooms and cook for 5 minutes more. Add red pepper and sauté for 2 minutes. Stir in tomatoes, parsley, 1 teaspoon salt, and ½ teaspoon black pepper. Add chicken and simmer over low heat for 10 minutes.

3. Cook and drain pasta. Preheat oven to 400°F.

4. Grease a 13″ × 9″ lasagna pan. Smear several tablespoons of tomato sauce (without large chunks of chicken or vegetables) across bottom. Line bottom with a layer of pasta, making sure noodles touch but do not overlap. Spread 1 cup sauce over pasta and sprinkle with ⅔ cup cheese. Repeat layering of pasta, sauce, and cheese four more times. For the sixth layer, sprinkle remaining 1 cup cheese over noodles.

5. Bake lasagna until cheese turns golden brown in spots and sauce is bubbling, about 20 minutes. Remove pan from oven, let lasagna settle for 5 minutes, and serve immediately.

Lasagna with Sausage and Ricotta

Creamy ricotta is matched with a rich sausage and tomato sauce to create a hearty and satisfying dish. Hot Italian sausage can be used instead of sweet.

SERVES 6–8

3 tablespoons olive oil
¼ cup finely minced onion
1 carrot, minced
1 rib celery, minced
1½ pounds sweet Italian sausage
½ cup dry white wine
3 cups canned crushed tomatoes
1 tablespoon minced fresh oregano leaves
1 teaspoon salt
½ teaspoon freshly ground black pepper
1 recipe Egg Pasta **or** ***Spinach Pasta (see Index)*** **or** ***18 dried lasagna noodles***
2 cups ricotta cheese
¼ cup warm water
1 cup freshly grated Parmesan cheese
1 tablespoon unsalted butter, diced

1. Heat olive oil in a large saucepan. Add onion and sauté over medium heat until translucent, about 5 minutes. Add carrot and celery and sauté until slightly softened, about 5 minutes.

2. Raise heat to medium-high and squeeze sausage from casings directly into saucepan. Use a fork to break it into small pieces. Cook until sausage is browned, about 5 minutes. Add wine and simmer until alcohol evaporates, about 5 minutes. Add tomatoes, oregano, salt, and pepper and simmer gently until sauce thickens, about 30 minutes. Taste for salt and set aside.

3. Cook and drain pasta. Preheat oven to 400°F. Mix ricotta and warm water until smooth.

4. Grease 13″ × 9″ lasagna pan. Line bottom with a layer of pasta, making sure noodles touch but do not overlap. Use a plastic spatula to cover noodles with ⅓ cup ricotta mixture. Spread 1 cup tomato sauce over ricotta and sprinkle with 2 tablespoons Parmesan. Repeat layering of pasta, ricotta, tomato sauce, and Parmesan four more times. For the sixth layer, spread remaining ⅓ cup ricotta over noodles and sprinkle with remaining 6 tablespoons Parmesan. Dot with diced butter.

5. Bake lasagna until top turns golden brown in spots and sauce is bubbling, about 20 minutes. Remove pan from oven, let lasagna settle for 5 minutes, and serve.

Cook's Note: Two tablespoons minced fresh basil or parsley may be substituted for the oregano.

Lasagna "Paglia e Fieno"

Paglia e fieno, *Italian for "straw and hay," refers to a classic country pasta dish made with egg (the color of straw) and spinach (the color of hay) fettuccine. The creamy sauce usually contains mushrooms and ham. I have adapted this classic by using the same sauce with both egg and spinach lasagna noodles. The results are striking.*

SERVES 6–8

4 tablespoons unsalted butter
3 large shallots, minced fine
2 pounds white mushrooms, trimmed and sliced thin
1 teaspoon salt
½ teaspoon freshly ground black pepper
½ pound baked ham, cut into ¼" × ½" strips
¼ cup minced fresh parsley leaves
9 dried egg lasagna noodles
9 dried spinach lasagna noodles
1½ cups Béchamel Sauce (see Index)
1 cup freshly grated Parmesan cheese

1. Heat butter in a saucepan large enough to hold all the mushrooms. Add shallots and sauté over medium heat until golden, about 3 minutes. Stir in mushrooms, salt, and pepper and sauté until mushrooms have wilted and thrown off their liquid, about 7 minutes. To ensure even cooking, occasionally pull mushrooms from bottom of pan over the top mushrooms.

2. Add ham and cook, stirring constantly to separate strips, for 2 minutes. Remove pan from heat and stir in parsley. Set aside. (At this point several tablespoons of liquid from the mushrooms should still be in the pan. Use this

liquid along with sauce when making the lasagna. However, if there is more than ¼ cup, continue heating sauce to cook off more of the mushroom juice.)

3. Cook and drain both kinds of pasta. Preheat oven to 400°F.

4. Grease a 13″ × 9″ lasagna pan. Smear 3 tablespoons béchamel across bottom. Line bottom with a layer of egg pasta, making sure noodles touch but do not overlap. Spread ¾ cup mushroom mixture over noodles and drizzle with 3 tablespoons béchamel. Sprinkle with 2 tablespoons cheese. Cover with a layer of spinach noodles. Repeat steps, adding mushrooms, béchamel, and cheese. Alternate egg and spinach layers to make a total of three egg and two spinach layers. For the sixth layer, coat remaining spinach noodles with 6 tablespoons béchamel and sprinkle with remaining 6 tablespoons cheese.

5. Bake lasagna until top turns golden brown in spots and sauce is bubbling, about 20 minutes. Remove pan from oven, let lasagna settle for 5 minutes, and serve.

Cook's Note: If you have time, try making this recipe with fresh Egg Pasta and Spinach Pasta (see Index). You will need just half a recipe of each.

Nana's Classic Lasagna with Sausages and Braciole

This meal recalls festive Sunday dinners with my grandparents. My mother's mother learned this classic from her mother, a native of Calabria. Sausages and braciole—thin pieces of round steak wrapped around a mixture of fresh herbs, grated cheese, pine nuts, and raisins—are browned and then simmered in tomato puree. The meat is set aside, and the tomato sauce is used in the lasagna, along with fresh pasta, meatballs, slices of mozzarella, and grated Pecorino Romano cheese. This hearty, sauce-driven lasagna takes all day to prepare but is worth the effort. It should be prepared in a deep disposable aluminum roasting pan.

SERVES 12–15

FOR THE BRACIOLE

3 pounds round steak prepared for braciole (ask your butcher to do this or cut top round into long pieces about ¼ inch thick)
Olive oil for brushing meat
Salt and freshly ground black pepper to taste
2 large cloves garlic, minced fine
½ cup raisins
½ cup pine nuts
½ cup chopped fresh parsley leaves
¼ cup chopped fresh basil leaves
⅓ cup freshly grated Pecorino Romano cheese

FOR THE SAUSAGES AND TOMATO SAUCE

½ cup olive oil
3 large cloves garlic, peeled
2 pounds mixed hot and sweet Italian sausage, cut into pieces about 3 inches long
¼ cup chopped fresh parsley leaves
Several fresh basil sprigs
1 tablespoon dried oregano leaves
5 29-ounce cans tomato puree
1 tablespoon salt
1 teaspoon freshly ground black pepper

FOR THE LASAGNA

1 recipe meatballs from Nana's Lasagna with Tiny Meatballs (recipe follows)
1 recipe Egg Pasta (see Index)
3 pounds mozzarella cheese, sliced thin
¾ pound freshly grated Pecorino Romano or Parmesan cheese

1. Lay prepared round steak flat on a large work surface. Brush tops of meat with oil and sprinkle with salt and pepper. Combine garlic, raisins, pine nuts, herbs, and cheese and spread mixture evenly over meat. Beginning at the narrow ends, roll up pieces of meat and secure with metal picks. Secure ends as well to prevent filling from leaking. Set braciole aside.

2. Heat ½ cup oil in a deep, heavy saucepan that holds at least 8 quarts. Add whole garlic cloves and sauté over medium heat until golden brown, about 5 minutes. Remove and discard garlic and add sausages. Sauté over medium heat until nicely browned, about 30 minutes. Remove sausages from pan and set aside.

3. Add rolled meat to oil in pan and sauté, turning once or twice, until well browned, 35 to 40 minutes. Add parsley, basil, oregano, tomato puree, salt, and pepper. Partially cover to prevent splattering and simmer gently, stirring occasionally, until meat is very tender, about 2 hours. Add cooked sausages and simmer for another 30 minutes. Correct seasonings. Remove braciole and sausage. Set aside with about 1 cup tomato sauce. Remove basil sprigs from sauce and discard.

4. Make meatballs by following steps 1 and 2 in the next recipe. Add meatballs to tomato sauce and simmer gently for 5 minutes to blend flavors. Set meatballs and sauce aside.

5. Cook and drain pasta. Preheat oven to 375°F.

6. Grease a deep 16″ × 11″ roasting pan. Smear ½ tomato sauce (without large meatballs) across bottom. Line bottom with a layer of pasta, making sure noodles touch but do not overlap. Cover pasta with a layer of mozzarella slices. Spread one-quarter of remaining tomato sauce and meatballs (about 2½ cups) over mozzarella and sprinkle with one-quarter of grated Romano cheese (about ¾ cup). Repeat layering of pasta, mozzarella, tomato sauce with meatballs, and grated Romano cheese three more times.

7. Bake lasagna until sauce is bubbling and a knife inserted in center comes out very hot, about 45 minutes. (If at any time the top begins to dry out or burn, cover pan with foil.) Meanwhile, heat sausages and braciole in their tomato sauce. Remove lasagna pan from oven, cover, and let settle for 10 minutes. Remove metal picks from braciole and slice into pieces about 1½ inches thick. Serve lasagna with sausages and braciole passed in separate bowls.

Nana's Lasagna with Tiny Meatballs

This simplified version of my grandmother's classic lasagna is just as delicious but a lot less work. Instead of rolling out meatballs one at a time, my grandmother simply pinches off pieces of meat and places them directly in the pan. This technique is fast and yields flat meatballs of various sizes (all smaller than a grape) that will fit snugly between layers of pasta. The addition of ground pork enriches the meatballs and gives the lasagna a flavor reminiscent of southern Italy.

SERVES 6–8

1 pound ground round
⅓ pound ground pork
2 large eggs, lightly beaten
½ cup freshly grated Pecorino Romano **or** ***Parmesan cheese***
½ cup unseasoned bread crumbs
¼ cup minced fresh parsley leaves
¼ cup minced fresh basil leaves
1½ teaspoons salt
½ teaspoon freshly ground black pepper
Olive oil for frying meatballs
1 recipe Quick Tomato Sauce (see Index)
1 recipe Egg Pasta **or** ***Spinach Pasta (see Index)*** **or** ***18 dried lasagna noodles***
1 pound mozzarella cheese, shredded

1. Combine beef, pork, eggs, cheese, bread crumbs, herbs, salt, and pepper in a large bowl. Mix well with your hands.

2. Heat about ¼ inch of olive oil in a large skillet. Take a handful of the meatball mixture and work directly over the pan. Break off pieces about the size of grapes and place in the hot oil. It's best if the pieces are a bit flat (they will lie better in the lasagna); they can vary in size. Add as many meatballs as will fit comfortably in a single layer. Fry meatballs, turning several times, until nicely browned, about 4 minutes. Use a slotted spoon to transfer cooked meatballs to a platter lined with paper towels. Repeat, adding more oil as needed, until all of the meatballs have been cooked.

3. Add meatballs to prepared tomato sauce and heat through for several minutes. Remove pan from heat.

4. Cook and drain pasta. Preheat oven to 400°F.

5. Grease a 13″ × 9″ lasagna pan. Smear several tablespoons of tomato sauce (without large meatballs) across bottom. Line bottom with a layer of pasta, making sure noodles touch but do not overlap. Spread ¾ cup meatballs and tomato sauce mixture over pasta and sprinkle with ⅔ cup cheese. Repeat layering of pasta, meatballs and sauce, and cheese four more times. For the sixth layer, cover pasta with remaining 1 cup cheese.

6. Bake lasagna until cheese turns golden brown in spots and sauce is bubbling, about 20 minutes. Remove pan from oven, let lasagna settle for 5 minutes, and serve.

Cook's Note: The meatballs can be made with 1⅓ pounds beef and no pork if desired.

Sicilian-Style Lasagna with Cauliflower and Green Olives

Anchovies, green olives, and tomatoes enliven this cauliflower-based sauce inspired by the flavors of Sicily. I like colossal Sicilian green olives, but other varieties in brine can be used in this recipe. If you opt for smaller olives, add at least 15 or 20 to the sauce.

SERVES 6–8

1 recipe Quick Tomato Sauce (see Index), salt omitted
1 small head (about 2 pounds) cauliflower
4 flat anchovy fillets, minced
10 very large green olives, pitted and chopped
Salt to taste
1 recipe Egg Pasta* or *Herb Pasta (see Index)* or *18 dried lasagna noodles
¾ pound mozzarella cheese, shredded

1. Set prepared sauce aside in a large saucepan.

2. Bring several quarts of water to a boil in a large pot. Trim and discard outer leaves from cauliflower. Remove core and break cauliflower into small florets. Slice florets into ½-inch-thick pieces. You should have about 4 cups. Add cauliflower to boiling water and cook until crisp-tender, about 4 minutes. Do not let cauliflower become mushy.

3. Drain cauliflower and add slices to reserved tomato sauce along with anchovies and olives. Simmer sauce gently for about 15 minutes to allow flavors to blend. Taste for salt (if olives are salty, the sauce may not need any) and set aside.

4. Cook and drain pasta. Preheat oven to 400°F.

5. Grease a 13″ × 9″ lasagna pan. Smear 3 tablespoons tomato sauce (without large pieces of cauliflower or olives) across bottom. Line bottom with a layer of pasta, making sure noodles touch but do not overlap. Smear ¾ cup sauce over pasta and sprinkle with ½ cup cheese. Repeat layering of pasta, sauce, and cheese four more times. For the sixth layer, cover pasta with remaining ¾ cup sauce and remaining ¾ cup cheese.

6. Bake lasagna until cheese turns golden brown in places and sauce is bubbling, about 20 minutes. Remove pan from oven, let lasagna settle for 5 minutes, and serve.

Lasagna with Chicken, Prosciutto, and Spinach

Chicken, ham, and spinach are paired with a delicate béchamel sauce and Parmesan cheese to create this refined but simple dish.

SERVES 6–8

½ pound fresh spinach, stems removed, **or** ***1 10-ounce package frozen chopped spinach***
3 tablespoons olive oil
1 small onion, chopped
3 cloves garlic, minced
3 ounces prosciutto **or** ***baked ham, cut into ½-inch squares***
1 pound skinless, boneless chicken breasts, fat trimmed, cut crosswise into ½-inch-wide strips
1 teaspoon salt
½ teaspoon freshly ground black pepper
⅓ cup dry white wine
2 cups canned crushed tomatoes
1 recipe Egg Pasta **or** ***Spinach Pasta (see Index)*** **or** ***18 dried lasagna noodles***
1½ cups Béchamel Sauce (see Index)
1 cup freshly grated Parmesan cheese

1. Bring several quarts of water to a boil in a medium-size pot. Add fresh spinach and cook for 1 minute. Drain spinach well. When cool, chop coarse and set aside. If you're using frozen spinach, cook it in boiling water, drain well, and reserve for use in the sauce.

2. Heat oil in a large saucepan. Add onion and sauté over medium heat until translucent, about 5 minutes. Stir in garlic and prosciutto and cook, stirring frequently to separate pieces of ham, for about 2 minutes.

3. Raise heat to medium-high, add chicken, salt, and pepper, and cook, stirring often, until meat is seared, about 3 minutes. Add wine and simmer until chicken is cooked through and most of the wine has evaporated, about 3 minutes more. Add reserved spinach and stir to distribute evenly. Add tomatoes and bring mixture to a boil. Reduce heat and simmer gently until sauce is quite thick, about 30 minutes. Taste for salt and set sauce aside.

4. Cook and drain pasta. Preheat oven to 400°F.

5. Grease a 13″ × 9″ lasagna pan. Smear 3 tablespoons béchamel across bottom. Line bottom with a layer of pasta, making sure noodles touch but do not overlap. Spread ¾ cup tomato sauce over pasta. Drizzle with 3 tablespoons béchamel and sprinkle with 2 tablespoons cheese. Repeat layering of pasta, tomato sauce, béchamel, and cheese four more times. For the sixth layer, cover pasta with 6 tablespoons béchamel and sprinkle with remaining 6 tablespoons cheese.

6. Bake lasagna until top turns golden brown in spots and sauce is bubbling, about 20 minutes. Remove pan from oven, let lasagna settle for 5 minutes, and serve.

Hearty Potato Lasagna with Kale and Chorizo

A cross between a potato gratin and lasagna, this dish relies on thin slices of prebaked potatoes to take the place of pasta. The combination of kale, spicy sausage, and cheese in the filling will please even finicky eaters.

SERVES 8

6 large (about 3 pounds) baking potatoes
5 tablespoons olive oil
1 tablespoon minced garlic
1 tablespoon minced fresh oregano leaves
½ teaspoon salt
½ teaspoon freshly ground black pepper
1 pound kale, stems removed
1 onion, chopped
¾ pound chorizo* or *hot Italian sausage
1½ cups ricotta cheese
½ pound mozzarella cheese, shredded

1. Scrub potatoes under cold running water, but do not peel. Cut lengthwise into ¼-inch-thick slices. Discard first and last slices (the ones with skin on one side) from each potato. Place potato slices in a large bowl and preheat oven to 400°F.

2. Combine ¼ cup of the olive oil, the garlic, oregano, salt, and pepper in a small bowl. Pour mixture over potatoes and toss gently with your hands to make sure each potato slice is coated with oil.

3. Grease two large jelly roll pans. Lay potato slices on pans, making sure they do not overlap. Cover pans tightly with aluminum foil and bake for 30 minutes. Remove pans from oven, uncover, and cool. Do not turn off oven.

4. Boil kale in several quarts of lightly salted water for 4 minutes. Drain, cool, and chop kale into very small pieces.

5. Heat remaining tablespoon of oil in a large saucepan. Add onion and sauté over medium heat until translucent, about 5 minutes. Squeeze sausage from casings directly into saucepan. Use a fork or heavy spoon to break sausage into small pieces. Cook until browned, about 5 minutes. Stir in kale and heat through for a minute or so. Remove pan from heat, cool slightly, and stir in ricotta.

6. Grease a 13″ × 9″ lasagna pan. Line bottom with a third of the potato slices, making sure they touch but do not overlap. Spoon half the sausage and kale mixture over the potatoes. Sprinkle with a third of the mozzarella. Make a second layer with a third of the potatoes, remaining sausage and kale mixture, and a third of the mozzarella. Top with remaining potatoes and sprinkle with remaining mozzarella.

7. Bake lasagna until cheese turns golden brown in spots, 20 to 25 minutes. Remove pan from oven, let lasagna settle for 5 minutes, and serve.

Cook's Note: Chorizo is a spicy Spanish sausage. Hot Italian sausage may be used instead.

Potato Lasagna with Spinach, Mushrooms, and Gruyère

Bacon lends a wonderful smokiness to a mixture of fresh spinach, mushrooms, and Gruyère cheese. Swiss cheese can be substituted, and vegetarians can omit the bacon.

SERVES 8

6 large (about 3 pounds) baking potatoes
5 tablespoons olive oil
1 tablespoon finely minced garlic
½ teaspoon salt
½ teaspoon freshly ground black pepper
1 onion, chopped fine
½ pound bacon, cut into ½-inch squares
½ pound fresh white mushrooms, trimmed and sliced thin
1½ pounds spinach, stems removed
1½ cups ricotta cheese
½ pound Gruyère cheese, shredded

1. Scrub potatoes under cold running water, but do not peel. Cut lengthwise into ¼-inch-thick slices. Discard first and last slices (the ones with skin on one side) from each potato. Place potatoes in a large bowl and preheat oven to 400°F.

2. Combine ¼ cup of the olive oil with garlic, salt, and pepper in a small bowl. Pour mixture over potatoes and toss gently with your hands to make sure each potato slice is coated with oil.

3. Grease two large jelly roll pans. Lay potato slices on pans, making sure they do not overlap. Cover pans tightly with aluminum foil and bake for 30 minutes. Remove pans from oven, uncover, and cool. Do not turn off oven.

4. Heat remaining tablespoon of oil in a large, deep saucepan. Add onion and sauté over medium heat until translucent, about 5 minutes. Add bacon and fry until crisp, about 7 minutes. Add mushrooms and continue cooking until they throw off their juices, about 5 minutes. Stir in spinach, cover, and cook until wilted, 2 or 3 minutes more. Uncover and cook off any liquid that has accumulated in the pan. Remove pan from heat and cool slightly. Stir in ricotta and set mixture aside.

5. Grease a 13″ × 9″ lasagna pan. Line bottom of pan with a third of the potato slices, making sure they touch but do not overlap. Spoon half the spinach mixture over the potatoes. Sprinkle with a third of the Gruyère. Make a second layer with a third of the potatoes, remaining spinach mixture, and a third of the Gruyère. Top with remaining potatoes and sprinkle with remaining cheese.

6. Bake lasagna until cheese turns golden brown in spots, 20 to 25 minutes. Remove pan from oven, let lasagna settle for 5 minutes, and serve.

Polenta Lasagna with Chianti Meat Sauce

This meat sauce is enriched with Chianti, a hearty red wine from Tuscany, and then paired with Asiago, a slightly piquant cow's milk cheese that is creamy and crumbly at the same time. Parmesan or Pecorino Romano cheese may be substituted.

SERVES 8

2 tablespoons olive oil
2 tablespoons unsalted butter
1 small onion, minced
1 carrot, minced
1 rib celery, minced
½ pound ground beef
½ pound ground pork
1 teaspoon salt
½ teaspoon freshly ground black pepper
1 cup Chianti **or** ***other dry red wine***
1 28-ounce can crushed tomatoes
¼ cup minced fresh parsley leaves
1 recipe Polenta (see Index)
½ pound freshly grated Asiago **or**
Parmesan cheese

1. Heat oil and butter in a large saucepan. Add onion and sauté over medium heat until translucent, about 5 minutes. Add carrot and celery and cook until softened, about 5 minutes more. Add beef, pork, salt, and pepper and use a spoon or fork to crumble the meat. Cook just until the meat loses its red color, about 4 minutes.

2. Add wine and tomatoes and bring sauce to a boil. Reduce heat and simmer gently until sauce loses its soupy consistency and thickens somewhat, about 40 minutes. Stir in parsley and adjust salt and pepper. Set aside.

3. Pour half of the prepared polenta into a greased 13″ × 9″ lasagna pan and the other half onto a greased 13″ × 9″ baking sheet. Cool polenta for about 10 minutes. Meanwhile, preheat oven to 425°F.

4. Spread half of the meat sauce over polenta in lasagna pan and sprinkle with half of the cheese. Cut polenta on the baking sheet into four pieces and transfer pieces one at a time to the lasagna pan, making sure the first layer is completely covered. Spread remaining meat sauce over second layer of polenta and sprinkle with remaining cheese.

5. Bake lasagna until cheese turns golden brown in spots and sauce is bubbling, about 20 minutes. Remove pan from oven, let lasagna settle for 10 minutes, and serve.

Cook's Note: Unlike lasagna made with pasta, this dish cannot be assembled ahead of time. However, the meat sauce and polenta can be prepared separately a day in advance. Refrigerate sauce in an airtight container and reheat before using. Wrap the polenta tightly in plastic and refrigerate overnight. Let the polenta come to room temperature before assembling the dish.

-5-

VEGETARIAN DELIGHTS

Lasagna Primavera
Lasagna with Asparagus, Basil, and Parmesan
Lasagna with Broccoli, Carrots, and Red Bell Pepper
Lasagna with Spring Greens and Wild Mushrooms
Lasagna with Eggplant, Basil, and Tomatoes
Lasagna with Zucchini and Shiitake Mushrooms
Lasagna with Creamy Spinach and Gorgonzola
Lasagna with Spicy Cauliflower Sauce
Lasagna with Snow Peas, Mushrooms, and Tomatoes
Lasagna with Braised Cannellini Beans

Lasagna Primavera

Nothing says spring like this dish filled with fresh peas, summer squash, asparagus, broccoli, and tomatoes. Feel free to use any other vegetables that look good at the market, including zucchini, green beans, and fresh fava beans. The secret to this dish is blanching each vegetable separately and then combining them to make an exciting sauce with contrasting flavors and textures.

SERVES 6–8

1½ cups shelled fresh peas
1 small yellow squash, diced small
8 thin asparagus, trimmed (see page 73)
1½ cups chopped broccoli florets
6 tablespoons olive oil
1 tablespoon finely minced garlic
½ pound fresh white mushrooms, trimmed and sliced thin
Salt and freshly ground black pepper to taste
1½ pounds plum tomatoes, peeled, seeded, and chopped (see page 23)
½ cup chopped fresh basil leaves
1 receipe Egg Pasta* or *Herb Pasta (see Index)* or *18 dried lasagna noodles
1 recipe Béchamel Sauce (see Index)
1½ cups freshly grated Parmesan cheese

1. Cook peas, squash, asparagus, and broccoli separately in boiling water for 1 minute each, drain, refresh in cold water, drain again, and set aside in a very large bowl. Once all the vegetables have been added to the bowl, drain off any excess water. Vegetable mixture should be very dry.

2. Heat 3 tablespoons of the olive oil in a large skillet. Add half of the garlic and sauté over medium heat until golden, about 2 minutes. Add mushrooms and cook until the liquid they throw off has evaporated, about 5 minutes. Season generously with salt and pepper and pour into bowl with vegetables.

3. Heat remaining 3 tablespoons oil in the empty skillet. Add remaining garlic and sauté over medium heat until golden, about 2 minutes. Add tomatoes, season generously with salt and pepper, and cook for about 3 minutes. Stir in basil and pour mixture into bowl with vegetables. Toss well and add salt and pepper to taste.

4. Cook and drain pasta. Preheat oven to 400°F.

5. Grease a 13″ × 9″ lasagna pan. Smear 3 tablespoons béchamel across bottom. Line bottom with a layer of pasta, making sure noodles touch but do not overlap. Spread 1 generous cup of the vegetable mixture over noodles. (There may be some liquid at the bottom of the bowl with the vegetables. If so, use a slotted spoon to scoop out the vegetables.) Drizzle 3 tablespoons béchamel over vegetables and sprinkle with 4 tablespoons cheese. Repeat layering of pasta, vegetables, béchamel, and cheese four more times. For the sixth layer, coat noodles with 6 tablespoons béchamel and sprinkle with remaining 4 tablespoons cheese.

6. Bake lasagna until top turns golden brown in places and sauce is bubbling, about 20 minutes. Remove pan from oven, let lasagna settle for 10 minutes, and serve.

Lasagna with Asparagus, Basil, and Parmesan

The asparagus needs to be cut into bite-size pieces that will fit snugly between layers of pasta and then blanched until crisp-tender. Refreshing the cooked asparagus in cold water stops the cooking process and keeps it firm. For an interesting spring variation, use ⅓ cup chopped fresh mint leaves instead of basil.

SERVES 6

1 gallon water
2½ pounds thin asparagus (see page 73)
Salt to taste
2 tablespoons unsalted butter
2 tablespoons olive oil
2 tablespoons finely minced garlic
½ teaspoon freshly ground black pepper
¾ cup chopped basil leaves
1 recipe Egg Pasta or Basil and Garlic Pasta (see Index) or 18 dried lasagna noodles
1¾ cups Béchamel Sauce (see Index)
1¼ cups freshly grated Parmesan cheese

1. Bring water to a boil in a large pot. Add trimmed asparagus pieces and salt and cook for 1 minute. Drain and refresh asparagus in a large bowl of cold water. Drain again and set aside.

2. Heat butter and oil in a large saucepan. Add garlic and sauté over medium heat until golden, about 2 minutes. Add asparagus, 1 teaspoon salt, and pepper and toss for about 1 minute. Remove pan from heat and stir in basil.

3. Cook and drain pasta. Preheat oven to 400°F.

4. Grease a 13″ × 9″ lasagna pan. Smear 3 tablespoons béchamel across bottom. Line bottom with a layer of pasta, making sure noodles touch but do not overlap. Spread 1 cup asparagus over noodles. Drizzle with ¼ cup béchamel and sprinkle with 3 tablespoons cheese. Repeat layering of pasta, asparagus, béchamel, and cheese four more times. For the sixth layer, coat noodles with 5 tablespoons béchamel and sprinkle with remaining 5 tablespoons cheese.

5. Bake lasagna until top turns golden brown in spots, about 20 minutes. Remove pan from oven, let lasagna settle for 5 minutes, and serve.

Trimming Asparagus

The tough ends of asparagus spears need to be removed for almost all recipes. They will snap off in just the right spot if you use this easy technique. Hold the middle of the stalk in one hand and wrap thumb and index finger of your other hand around the stem end about 1 inch from bottom. Gently bend to pull off tough end. Reserve stem ends for soup or discard. For lasagna recipes, asparagus pieces must be cut quite small. Thin spears should be halved lengthwise (larger spears quartered) and then cut on the bias into ½-inch pieces.

Lasagna with Broccoli, Carrots, and Red Bell Pepper

Separate layers of three colorful vegetables make this lasagna pleasing to the eyes as well as the taste buds. To speed the cooking of the vegetables, make sure they are cut into very small dice—no larger than ¼-inch pieces. Save this vegetarian feast (which is a bit more complicated than other recipes in this chapter) for special occasions and use fresh noodles if at all possible.

SERVES 6–8

4 tablespoons unsalted butter
6 cloves garlic, peeled and lightly crushed
1 pound carrots, cut into very small dice
¼ cup water
Salt to taste
¾ pound (2 small) red bell peppers, cut into very small dice
2 small bunches (about 2½ pounds) broccoli
1 recipe Egg Pasta* or *Herb Pasta (see Index)* or *18 dried lasagna noodles
2½ cups Béchamel Sauce (see Index)
1¾ cups freshly grated Parmesan cheese

1. Melt 1 tablespoon of the butter in a large skillet. Add 2 cloves of the crushed garlic and sauté over medium heat until light brown, about 5 minutes. Remove and discard garlic and add carrots and 2 tablespoons of the water. Sauté carrots, stirring occasionally, until tender but not mushy, 10 to 15 minutes. (The carrots should start to shrink in size and become lightly colored.) Set cooked carrots aside in a medium-size bowl and season with salt to taste.

2. Melt 1 tablespoon of the remaining butter in a clean skillet. Add 2 cloves of the crushed garlic and sauté over medium heat until light brown, about 5 minutes. Remove and discard garlic and add red bell pepper. Sauté, stirring

occasionally, until tender but not mushy, about 4 minutes. Set cooked red pepper aside in another medium-size bowl and season with salt to taste.

3. Trim broccoli florets (there should be about 6 cups) and boil in lightly salted water for 2 minutes. Drain, refresh in cold water, and drain again. Chop blanched broccoli into very small dice. Melt remaining 2 tablespoons butter in a clean saucepan. Add remaining 2 cloves crushed garlic and sauté over medium heat until light brown, about 5 minutes. Remove and discard garlic and add broccoli and remaining 2 tablespoons water. Sauté broccoli, stirring occasionally, until tender but not mushy, about 6 minutes. Set cooked broccoli aside in another medium-size bowl and season with salt to taste.

4. Cook and drain pasta. Preheat oven to 400°F.

5. Set ½ cup béchamel aside. Divide remaining sauce among the three bowls with vegetables, adding ¾ cup each to carrots and broccoli and ½ cup to bell peppers. Mix béchamel well with each vegetable and adjust salt if necessary.

6. Grease a 13″ × 9″ lasagna pan. Smear 3 tablespoons reserved béchamel across bottom. Line bottom with a layer of pasta, making sure noodles touch but do not overlap. Spread half of the broccoli mixture over noodles, making sure noodles are well coated with béchamel from broccoli mixture. Sprinkle with ¼ cup cheese and top with another layer of pasta. Cover second layer with half of the carrot mixture, again making sure noodles are well coated with béchamel from carrot mixture. Sprinkle with ¼ cup cheese and top with a third layer of pasta. Spread all of the pepper mixture over noodles and sprinkle with ¼ cup cheese. Use remaining broccoli and carrot mixtures to form fourth and fifth layers, sprinkling ¼ cup cheese over each layer. For the sixth layer, coat noodles with remaining reserved béchamel and sprinkle with remaining cheese.

7. Bake lasagna until top turns golden brown in spots and sauce is bubbling, about 15 minutes. Remove from oven, let lasagna settle for 5 minutes, and serve.

Lasagna with Spring Greens and Wild Mushrooms

This delicate but hearty combination is perfect when the weather has begun to warm up but there is still a chill in the air. Try to choose greens of different colors and flavors (red chard is especially attractive and tasty) for maximum appeal. However, as long as you have about 2½ pounds trimmed greens, any combination can be used.

SERVES 6

1½ pounds Swiss chard (preferably with red veins), stalks removed (you should have about ¾ pound leaves)
1¾ pounds escarole, cored and tough stalks removed (you should have about 1 pound leaves)
1 pound spinach, stems removed (you should have about ¾ pound leaves)
⅓ cup olive oil
1½ tablespoons finely minced garlic
1 pound fresh shiitake* or *other wild mushrooms (see page 81), stems removed and caps cut into ½-inch dice
1½ teaspoons salt
½ teaspoon freshly ground black pepper
1 recipe Egg Pasta* or *Herb Pasta (see Index)* or *18 dried lasagna noodles
1½ cups Béchamel Sauce (see Index)
1 cup freshly grated Parmesan cheese

1. Cook leaves from each green separately in several quarts of lightly salted boiling water. Swiss chard should cook for about 2 minutes and escarole and spinach for about 1 minute. Greens should be tender but not fully cooked. Drain

greens, cool, and squeeze out excess moisture with your hands. Chop coarse and set all the greens aside in one bowl.

2. Heat olive oil in a large saucepan. Add garlic and sauté over medium heat for about 1 minute. Add mushrooms and sauté, stirring occasionally, until they have cooked down and are soft, about 10 minutes. Stir in salt and pepper and then reserved greens. Mix well to combine ingredients, taste for salt, and set aside.

3. Cook and drain pasta. Preheat oven to 400°F.

4. Grease a 13″ × 9″ lasagna pan. Smear ¼ cup béchamel across bottom. Line bottom with a layer of pasta, making sure noodles touch but do not overlap. Spread 1 cup greens and mushroom mixture over pasta. Drizzle with 3 tablespoons béchamel and sprinkle with 2 tablespoons cheese. Repeat layering of pasta, greens, béchamel, and cheese four more times. For the sixth layer, coat pasta with 5 tablespoons béchamel and sprinkle with remaining 6 tablespoons cheese.

5. Bake lasagna until top turns golden brown in spots, about 20 minutes. Remove pan from oven, let lasagna settle for 5 minutes, and serve.

Lasagna with Eggplant, Basil, and Tomatoes

❦

This hearty dish is typical of the southern region of Italy. Golden slices of eggplant are layered with a chunky fresh tomato sauce redolent of garlic and basil. Mozzarella cheese gives the dish its creaminess.

SERVES 8

2 (about 2½ pounds) eggplants
Coarse salt
Vegetable oil for frying eggplant
1 recipe Egg Pasta* or *Basil and Garlic Pasta (see Index)* or *18 dried lasagna noodles
1 recipe Fresh Tomato Sauce (see Index)
1 pound mozzarella cheese, shredded

1. Cut the eggplant lengthwise into ¼-inch-thick slices. Discard the first and last slices (those with skin on one side). Spread several layers of paper towels on a countertop. Place eggplant slices on paper, sprinkle lightly with coarse salt, and cover with more paper towels. Let sit for about 1 hour, gently pressing eggplant occasionally to squeeze out juices. Wipe moisture and visible salt from eggplant with clean paper towels and set aside.

2. Heat ½ inch of oil in a large skillet. When oil is hot, slide several eggplant slices into pan and cook over medium-high heat until browned on the bottom, about 3 minutes. Flip and continue frying until the other side is golden brown. Transfer slices to a baking sheet lined with paper towels. Repeat until all the slices are fried.

3. Cook and drain pasta. Preheat oven to 400°F.

4. Grease a 13″ × 9″ lasagna pan. Smear 2 tablespoons tomato sauce across bottom. Line bottom with a layer of pasta, making sure noodles touch but do not overlap. Spread ½ cup tomato sauce over noodles. Cover sauce with four or five slices of eggplant and sprinkle with ⅔ cup cheese. Repeat layering of pasta, tomato sauce, eggplant, and cheese four more times. For the sixth layer, smear remaining sauce over noodles and sprinkle with remaining 1 cup cheese.

5. Bake lasagna until cheese turns golden brown in places and sauce is bubbling, about 20 minutes. Remove pan from oven, let lasagna settle for 5 minutes, and serve.

Lasagna with Zucchini and Shiitake Mushrooms

For this dish, zucchini and shiitake mushrooms are cooked and layered separately so that they retain their individual flavors. A delicate shallot-based tomato sauce ties the two together. There should be three layers with zucchini, two with mushrooms, and one (for the top) with just sauce and cheese. If shiitake mushrooms are unavailable, use an equal amount of any fresh wild mushrooms (see "Wild About Mushrooms") or 1½ pounds cultivated mushrooms.

SERVES 6–8

5 tablespoons unsalted butter
1 pound shiitake mushrooms, stems removed and caps cut into ¼-inch dice
2 teaspoons minced fresh thyme leaves
2 teaspoons salt
¾ teaspoon freshly ground black pepper
2 pounds zucchini, cut into ¼-inch dice
¼ cup finely minced shallots
1 28-ounce can crushed tomatoes
1 recipe Egg Pasta* or *Herb Pasta (see Index)* or *18 dried lasagna noodles
1 pound mozzarella cheese, shredded

1. Heat 2 tablespoons of the butter in a large saucepan. Add mushrooms and sauté over medium heat until tender, about 5 minutes. Transfer mushrooms to a bowl and stir in 1 teaspoon of the thyme, ¾ teaspoon of the salt, and ¼ teaspoon of the pepper. Set aside.

2. Heat 1 tablespoon of the remaining butter in a clean large saucepan. Add zucchini, remaining thyme, ¾ teaspoon of the remaining salt, and ¼ teaspoon of the remaining pepper and sauté over medium heat until zucchini is tender and liquid thrown off by vegetables has evaporated, about 10 minutes. Transfer mixture to another bowl and set aside.

3. Heat remaining 2 tablespoons butter in a medium-size saucepan. Add shallots and sauté over medium heat until wilted, about 2 minutes. Do not let shallots brown. Add tomatoes, remaining ½ teaspoon salt, and remaining ¼ teaspoon pepper. Simmer over low heat until sauce thickens somewhat, about 10 minutes.

4. Cook and drain pasta. Preheat oven to 400°F.

5. Grease a 13″ × 9″ lasagna pan. Smear several tablespoons tomato sauce across bottom. Line bottom with a layer of pasta, making sure noodles touch but do not overlap. Spread a third of the zucchini mixture over noodles. Pour ⅓ cup tomato sauce over zucchini and sprinkle with ⅔ cup cheese. Top with another layer of pasta. Spread half of the mushrooms over pasta and top with another ⅓ cup tomato sauce and ⅔ cup cheese. Repeat layering of pasta, vegetables, tomato sauce, and cheese three more times, using zucchini for the third and fifth layers and mushrooms for the fourth layer. For the sixth layer, coat pasta with remaining ½ cup sauce and sprinkle with remaining 1 cup cheese.

6. Bake lasagna until cheese turns golden brown in spots and sauce is bubbling, about 20 minutes. Remove pan from oven, let lasagna settle for 5 minutes, and serve.

Wild About Mushrooms

Shiitake mushrooms are a particularly meaty variety with a pleasant woodsy flavor. Other wild mushrooms, such as cremini, chanterelles, trumpets, and morels, are equally delicious in lasagna recipes but usually more difficult to find. If you're using white button mushrooms (the most common mushroom sold in supermarkets), be sure to cook them until the liquid they have thrown off has evaporated. Meaty mushrooms like shiitakes will not throw off as much liquid, making them easier to work with as well as more flavorful.

Lasagna with Creamy Spinach and Gorgonzola

Garlic-infused spinach and a rich Gorgonzola sauce are a potent but delectable combination. Any blue cheese may be used, but I prefer the creaminess and flavor of Italian Gorgonzola.

SERVES 6

6 quarts water
1 tablespoon salt
2 pounds spinach, stems removed,* or *3 10-ounce packages frozen chopped spinach
⅓ cup olive oil
1 tablespoon finely minced garlic
½ teaspoon freshly ground black pepper
1 recipe Egg Pasta* or *Herb Pasta (see Index)* or *18 dried lasagna noodles
1¾ cups Béchamel Sauce (see Index)
6 ounces Gorgonzola* or *other blue cheese, crumbled

1. Bring water to a boil in a large stockpot. Add 2 teaspoons of the salt and some of the spinach leaves. Stir quickly to make room for more spinach in the pot. Continue stirring and adding more spinach until all the leaves are in the pot. Boil until spinach is tender but not fully cooked, about 2 minutes. Drain spinach, cool, and squeeze out excess moisture with your hands. Coarsely chop spinach and set it aside. If you're using frozen spinach, boil it in lightly salted water, drain, and reserve for use in filling.

2. Heat olive oil in a large saucepan. Add garlic and sauté over medium heat until golden, about 3 minutes. Stir in spinach, remaining 1 teaspoon salt, and pepper. Mix well to combine ingredients. Taste for salt and set mixture aside.

3. Cook and drain pasta. Preheat oven to 400°F.

4. With saucepan of prepared béchamel still on burner, stir in all but ¼ cup crumbled cheese. Continue stirring until béchamel is smooth and thick.

5. Grease a 13″ × 9″ lasagna pan. Smear 3 tablespoons béchamel across bottom. Line bottom with a layer of pasta, making sure noodles touch but do not overlap. Spread ¾ cup spinach evenly over noodles and drizzle with ¼ cup béchamel. Repeat layering of pasta, spinach, and béchamel four more times. For the sixth layer, coat pasta with remaining béchamel and sprinkle with reserved ¼ cup crumbled cheese.

6. Bake lasagna until top turns golden brown in spots and sauce is bubbling, about 20 minutes. Remove pan from oven, let lasagna settle for 5 minutes, and serve.

Lasagna with Spicy Cauliflower Sauce

Tiny pieces of sautéed cauliflower and onions melt into a spicy tomato sauce for this hearty vegetarian dish.

SERVES 6–8

1 large head (about 2½ pounds) cauliflower
⅓ cup olive oil
4 tablespoons unsalted butter
3 cloves garlic, peeled and lightly crushed
3 onions, sliced thin
1 recipe Quick Tomato Sauce (see Index), 1 teaspoon hot red pepper flakes added along with garlic and parsley used instead of basil
2 tablespoons chopped fresh parsley leaves
1 teaspoon salt or to taste
1 recipe Egg Pasta* or *Black Pepper Pasta (see Index)* or *18 dried lasagna noodles
1 pound mozzarella cheese, shredded

1. Remove outside leaves from cauliflower and core. Remove and discard stems. Finely chop florets (you should have about 6 cups) and set aside.

2. Heat oil and 2 tablespoons of the butter in a large skillet. Add cauliflower and garlic cloves and sauté over medium heat, stirring occasionally, until cauliflower is tender and lightly browned, about 20 minutes. Remove cauliflower from pan and set aside in a large bowl.

3. Add remaining 2 tablespoons butter to pan with garlic. Add onion slices and sauté, stirring occasionally, until completely wilted and lightly colored, about 12 minutes. Remove and discard garlic cloves. Scrape onions into bowl with cauliflower. Stir in tomato sauce, parsley, and salt and set aside.

4. Cook and drain pasta. Preheat oven to 400°F.

5. Grease a 13″ × 9″ lasagna pan. Smear 2 tablespoons tomato sauce (without large chunks of cauliflower or onions) across bottom. Line bottom with a layer of pasta, making sure noodles touch but do not overlap. Spread 1 cup sauce over noodles and sprinkle with ⅔ cup cheese. Repeat layering of pasta, sauce, and cheese four more times. For the sixth layer, cover noodles with remaining 1 cup sauce and remaining 1 cup cheese.

6. Bake lasagna until cheese turns golden brown in spots and sauce is bubbling, about 20 minutes. Remove pan from oven, let lasagna settle for 5 minutes, and serve.

Lasagna with Snow Peas, Mushrooms, and Tomatoes

This lasagna features alternating layers of snow peas and mushrooms that have been enriched with a tomato-basil béchamel. Snow peas have the flavor of fresh spring peas but are sold throughout the year. When available, an equal amount of shelled peas can be substituted.

SERVES 6–8

2 tablespoons unsalted butter
3 tablespoons minced shallot
1 pound snow peas, trimmed and shredded (see Cook's Note)
¼ cup dry white wine
Salt and freshly ground black pepper to taste
10 ounces fresh white mushrooms, trimmed and sliced thin
1 pound plum tomatoes, peeled, seeded, and chopped (see page 23)
¼ cup chopped fresh basil leaves
1½ cups Béchamel Sauce (see Index)
1 recipe Egg Pasta* or *Spinach Pasta (see Index)* or *18 dried lasagna noodles
1 cup freshly grated Parmesan cheese

1. Heat 1 tablespoon of the butter in a nonstick skillet. Add 1½ tablespoons of the shallot and sauté over medium heat until golden, about 3 minutes. Raise heat to medium-high and add snow peas and wine. Toss peas several times and cook until tender but not mushy, about 5 minutes. Season with salt and pepper and set aside in a medium-size bowl.

2. Heat remaining 1 tablespoon butter in a clean nonstick skillet. Add remaining shallot and sauté over medium heat until golden, about 3 minutes. Raise

heat to medium-high and add mushrooms. Cook until mushrooms have wilted and the liquid they have thrown off has mostly evaporated, about 7 minutes. Season with salt and pepper and set aside in a medium-size bowl.

3. Stir tomatoes and basil into prepared béchamel. Pour 1 cup tomato béchamel into bowl with peas. Mix well and taste for salt and pepper. Pour another cup of tomato béchamel into bowl with mushrooms. Mix well and adjust salt and pepper. Set remaining ½ cup tomato béchamel aside.

4. Cook and drain pasta. Preheat oven to 400°F.

5. Grease a 13″ × 9″ lasagna pan. Smear several tablespoons tomato béchamel across bottom. Line bottom with a layer of pasta, making sure noodles touch but do not overlap. Spread a third of the snow pea mixture over pasta, making sure noodles are well coated with béchamel from pea mixture. Sprinkle with 2 tablespoons cheese. Cover with another layer of pasta. Smear half of the mushroom mixture over noodles and sprinkle with 2 tablespoons cheese. Repeat process, making third and fifth layers with snow peas and fourth layer with mushrooms. For the sixth layer, coat noodles with remaining tomato béchamel and sprinkle with remaining 6 tablespoons cheese.

6. Bake lasagna until top turns golden brown in spots and sauce is bubbling, about 20 minutes. Remove pan from oven, let lasagna settle for 5 minutes, and serve immediately.

Cook's Note: Trim snow peas by pulling on the feathery end and removing it along with the stringy fiber that runs along the top of the snow pea. To shred, cut peas crosswise into pieces about ¼-inch wide.

Lasagna with Braised Cannellini Beans

This dish is the perfect marriage of legume and grain. Canned beans may be used instead of dried, but they are sometimes quite salty and mushy. To reduce the saltiness, rinse them under cold water before adding to the sauce and add salt sparingly with the tomatoes.

SERVES 6–8

3 tablespoons olive oil
3 cloves garlic, minced fine
1 sprig fresh rosemary
3 cups canned crushed tomatoes
1 teaspoon salt
3 cups cooked cannellini beans (see Cook's Note)
1 recipe Egg Pasta* or *Spinach Pasta (see Index)* or *18 dried lasagna noodles
1¾ cups Béchamel Sauce (see Index)
1 cup freshly grated Parmesan cheese

1. Heat olive oil in a medium-size saucepan. Add garlic and rosemary and sauté until garlic is slightly colored, about 2 minutes. Add tomatoes and salt and simmer until sauce thickens slightly, about 5 minutes. Stir in beans and simmer for several minutes more to blend flavors. Taste for salt, remove and discard rosemary sprig, and set braised beans aside.

2. Cook and drain pasta. Preheat oven to 400°F.

3. Grease a 13″ × 9″ lasagna pan. Smear 3 tablespoons béchamel across bottom. Line bottom with a layer of pasta, making sure noodles touch but do not overlap. Spread 1 cup beans across noodles. Drizzle with ¼ cup béchamel and

sprinkle with 2 tablespoons cheese. Repeat layering of pasta, beans, béchamel, and cheese four more times. For the sixth layer, coat noodles with 5 tablespoons béchamel and remaining 6 tablespoons cheese.

4. Bake lasagna until top turns golden brown in places and sauce is bubbling, about 20 minutes. Remove pan from oven, let lasagna settle for 5 minutes, and serve.

Cook's Note: Place 1 cup (about ½ pound) dried cannellini beans in a large bowl and cover with 2 inches of water. Soak for 6 hours. Drain beans and place them in a deep pot. Cover with 2 quarts fresh water and add a bouquet garni (see "A Bunch of Flavor"). Do not add salt, because it will prevent beans from softening. Bring mixture to a boil and simmer gently until beans are tender but not mushy, about 1 hour. Drain, discard bouquet garni, and reserve beans.

A Bunch of Flavor

A bouquet garni is a bunch of aromatic herbs and vegetables used to boost flavor in soup, broth, or stock. Once the dish is cooked, the herbs are removed from the liquid and discarded, but they leave behind an unmistakable aroma and flavor. I usually start my bouquet garni with a rib of celery (with leaves if possible) or a piece of leek. Insert 4 whole cloves into the celery or leek. Place a sprig each of fresh parsley and fresh thyme as well as a dried bay leaf inside the rib or between the layers of leek. Secure them by tying a piece of kitchen twine or a long parsley stem around the celery rib or leek.

-6-

Sophisticated Showstoppers

Artichoke Lasagna with Tomato-Garlic Sauce
Lasagna with Dried Mushrooms and Parmesan
Lasagna with Veal Sauce and Saffron Béchamel
Elegant Pesto Lasagna
Lasagna with Baked Squash, Prosciutto, and Pine Nuts
Spring Lasagna with Leeks and Artichokes
Lasagna with Endive and Radicchio
Parsley Lasagna with Scallops and Bread Crumbs
Lasagna with Shrimp and Sun-Dried Tomato Sauce
Black Pepper Lasagna with Caramelized Onions and Pancetta
Chicken Liver Lasagna with Balsamic Vinegar and Tomatoes

Artichoke Lasagna with Tomato-Garlic Sauce

This procedure for cooking the artichokes guarantees that they will be incredibly tender and delicious. Because artichokes are so bulky, this lasagna has five layers instead of the standard six.

SERVES 6–8

4 medium-size artichokes, trimmed (see "Working with Artichokes")
2 tablespoons unsalted butter
1 teaspoon salt
2 tablespoons olive oil
4 cloves garlic, minced
1 28-ounce can crushed tomatoes
¼ teaspoon freshly ground black pepper
1 recipe Egg Pasta* or *Herb Pasta (see Index)* or *15 dried lasagna noodles
1½ cups Béchamel Sauce (see Index)
1 cup freshly grated Parmesan cheese

1. Drain the prepared artichokes and place them in a large saucepan with butter and water to cover. Simmer over medium-high heat until artichokes are very tender and water evaporates completely, about 45 minutes. If water evaporates and artichokes are not completely cooked, add more water as needed. Transfer cooked artichokes to a bowl, season with ½ teaspoon of the salt, and set aside.

2. Heat olive oil in the same saucepan. Add garlic and sauté over medium heat until golden, about 2 minutes. Add tomatoes, remaining ½ teaspoon salt, and pepper and simmer over medium heat for 5 minutes. Return artichokes to pan, check seasonings, and simmer for 5 minutes. Set aside.

3. Cook and drain pasta. Preheat oven to 400°F.

4. Grease a 13″ × 9″ lasagna pan. Smear 3 tablespoons béchamel across bottom. Line bottom with a layer of pasta, making sure noodles touch but do not overlap. Spread 1 cup tomato-artichoke sauce over pasta. Drizzle 4 tablespoons béchamel over artichokes and sprinkle with 3 tablespoons cheese. Repeat layering of pasta, tomato-artichoke sauce, béchamel, and cheese three more times. For the fifth layer, coat noodles with 5 tablespoons béchamel and sprinkle with remaining ¼ cup cheese.

5. Bake lasagna until top layer turns golden brown in spots and sauce is bubbling, about 20 minutes. Remove pan from oven, let lasagna settle for 5 minutes, and serve.

Working with Artichokes

Beneath the tough exterior of an artichoke lies a creamy vegetable that is used often in Italian cooking. Since cut artichokes will turn black almost immediately, it is important to rub cut surfaces with lemon juice as you work. Also, it is best to prepare only one artichoke at a time.

Begin by squeezing half of a lemon into a large bowl filled with cold water. Add the lemon half to the bowl. Pull back the tough outer leaves on the first artichoke, snapping them off at the base. Remove several layers until the leaves are mostly pale green or yellow in color. Cut off the pointed leaf tops that are dark green. (You should trim about 1 inch from top.) Trim the end of the stem and use a vegetable peeler to remove the outside layer of skin from the stem. Quarter the artichokes.

The next step is to remove the fuzzy choke in the center of each artichoke quarter. Beginning at the stem end, slide a small, sharp knife under the choke and cut away from you and toward the leaf tips. Thinly slice cleaned quarters into four or five pieces and transfer them to the bowl with cold water and lemon. As soon as one artichoke has been cleaned and sliced, repeat the procedure with the next artichoke.

Lasagna with Dried Mushrooms and Parmesan

With both dried porcini and fresh button mushrooms, this earthy lasagna has a rich, almost meaty flavor, but of course it is vegetarian. Sharp Parmesan cheese is the perfect accent to this powerfully flavored sauce.

SERVES 6–8

2 ounces dried porcini mushrooms (see "Porcini")
2 cups warm water
5 tablespoons unsalted butter
2 tablespoons olive oil
1 onion, finely chopped
2½ pounds fresh white mushrooms, trimmed and sliced thin
¼ cup dry white wine
2 teaspoons salt
½ teaspoon freshly ground black pepper
1 tablespoon finely minced fresh oregano leaves
1 recipe Egg Pasta **or** ***Black Pepper Pasta (see Index)*** **or** ***18 dried lasagna noodles***
1½ cups Béchamel Sauce (see Index)
1 cup freshly grated Parmesan cheese

1. Place dried mushrooms in a small bowl and cover with the warm water. Soak until mushrooms are soft, about 30 minutes. Carefully lift mushrooms from bowl and place them in a wire strainer. Pick through and discard any foreign matter (such as twigs or stones) and rinse mushrooms under warm water. Finely chop the mushrooms and set aside. Line strainer with two layers of paper towels

and place it over a wide bowl. Pour soaking liquid through towel-lined strainer and reserve juices in bowl.

2. Heat 2 tablespoons of the butter and the oil in a very large saucepan. Add onion and sauté over medium heat until translucent, about 5 minutes. Add fresh mushrooms and white wine and stir until mushrooms have absorbed the oil and wine, about 1 minute. Continue cooking and stirring occasionally until mushrooms begin to throw off some liquid, about 5 minutes. Add salt and pepper and finish cooking mushrooms, about 3 minutes.

3. Add chopped porcini, strained soaking liquid, and oregano to pan. Raise heat to medium-high and simmer until sauce thickens and much of the liquid has evaporated, about 20 minutes. The mushrooms should be very juicy but not soupy. Swirl in remaining 3 tablespoons butter to thicken sauce. Taste for salt and pepper and set aside.

4. Cook and drain pasta. Preheat oven to 400°F.

5. Grease a 13″ × 9″ lasagna pan. Smear ¼ cup béchamel across bottom. Line bottom with a layer of pasta, making sure noodles touch but do not overlap. Spread 1 cup mushroom sauce over pasta. Drizzle with 3 tablespoons béchamel and sprinkle with 2 tablespoons cheese. Repeat layering of pasta, mushrooms, béchamel, and cheese four more times. For the sixth layer, generously coat pasta with 5 tablespoons béchamel and sprinkle with remaining 6 tablespoons cheese.

6. Bake lasagna until top turns golden brown in spots and sauce is bubbling, about 20 minutes. Remove pan from oven, let lasagna settle for 10 minutes, and serve.

Cook's Note: Do not use dried herbs to flavor this sauce. Substitute 2 tablespoons minced parsley if fresh oregano cannot be located.

Porcini

Porcini are wild mushrooms used frequently in Italian kitchens. Also known as cèpes, *fresh porcini are rarely sold in this country. Fortunately, the dried version captures the woodsy essence of these delicious mushrooms. Look for them in small packets (or loose) at gourmet stores and better supermarkets.*

Lasagna with Veal Sauce and Saffron Béchamel

Saffron tints béchamel a brilliant yellowish orange and provides an exciting contrast to the veal and tomato sauce. Use plain egg pasta, which will turn a lovely hue when coated with the béchamel.

SERVES 6–8

3 tablespoons olive oil
1 small onion, minced
1 small carrot, minced
1 small rib celery, minced
1 pound ground veal
1 tablespoon finely minced fresh sage leaves
1½ teaspoons salt
½ cup dry white wine
2 cups canned crushed tomatoes
⅛ teaspoon saffron threads (see "Saffron")
1½ cups Béchamel Sauce (see Index)
1 recipe Egg Pasta (see Index)* or *18 dried lasagna noodles
1 cup freshly grated Parmesan cheese

1. Heat olive oil in a large saucepan. Add onion and sauté over medium heat until wilted, about 3 minutes. Add carrot and celery and cook until softened, about 6 minutes. Raise heat to medium-high and add veal, sage, and salt. Use a fork or the back of a spoon to crumble meat into small pieces. Cook until veal loses its pink color, about 4 minutes.

2. Add wine and simmer until the alcohol aroma fades, about 3 minutes. Add tomatoes and simmer gently until sauce thickens, 30 to 40 minutes. Taste for salt and set aside.

3. Place a small skillet over low heat. When pan is warm, add saffron and toast until fragrant, about 30 seconds. Remove pan from heat and set aside.

4. Whisk toasted saffron into prepared béchamel as it is finishing cooking and thickening.

5. Cook and drain pasta. Preheat oven to 400°F.

6. Grease a 13″ × 9″ lasagna pan. Smear 3 tablespoons béchamel across bottom. Line bottom with a layer of pasta, making sure noodles touch but do not overlap. Spread ¾ cup veal sauce over noodles. Drizzle with 3 tablespoons béchamel and 2 tablespoons cheese. Repeat layering of pasta, veal sauce, béchamel, and cheese four more times. For the sixth layer, smear 6 tablespoons béchamel over noodles and sprinkle with remaining 6 tablespoons cheese.

7. Bake lasagna until top turns golden brown in spots and sauce is bubbling, about 20 minutes. Remove pan from oven, let lasagna settle for 5 minutes, and serve.

Saffron

Although extremely expensive (an ounce costs hundreds of dollars), saffron is also unusually potent. Look for Spanish saffron threads (it's usually the best) and don't be fooled by impostors made from marigolds or turmeric from Mexico or India. Quickly toasting saffron in a warm pan releases its full flavor.

Elegant Pesto Lasagna

Alternating layers of pesto and béchamel make this lasagna both simple and decadent. Homemade Spinach Pasta or Basil and Garlic Pasta will make an especially stunning presentation.

SERVES 6–8

3 cups tightly packed fresh basil leaves
3 garlic cloves, peeled
¼ cup pine nuts
½ cup olive oil
1 cup freshly grated Parmesan cheese
¼ cup ricotta cheese
1 teaspoon salt
½ teaspoon freshly ground black pepper
Spinach Pasta* or *Basil and Garlic Pasta (see Index for recipes and Cook's Note for quantities)* or *24 dried lasagna noodles
1½ cups Béchamel Sauce (see Index)

1. Place basil, garlic, and pine nuts in the work bowl of a food processor and grind, scraping down several times, until fine. With motor running, slowly pour olive oil through feed tube and process until smooth. Scrape pesto into a large bowl and stir in ¾ cup of the Parmesan along with the ricotta, salt, and pepper. Taste for seasonings and set aside.

2. Cook and drain pasta, reserving ¼ cup cooking liquid. Add reserved cooking water to pesto and stir until pesto is smooth and rather thin.

3. Preheat oven to 400°F.

4. Grease a 13″ × 9″ lasagna pan. Smear 3 tablespoons béchamel across bottom. Line bottom with a layer of pasta, making sure noodles touch but do not overlap. Use a plastic spatula to spread ⅓ cup pesto over noodles. Cover with a second layer of noodles. Evenly spread a generous ¼ cup béchamel sauce over these noodles. Repeat layering of noodles, pesto, noodles, and béchamel two more times. You should now have a total of six layers. Make a final pesto layer and then a layer with béchamel (the eighth layer) using the remaining ⅓ cup sauce to coat noodles. Sprinkle top with remaining ¼ cup Parmesan cheese.

5. Bake lasagna until top turns golden brown in spots and pesto is bubbling, about 15 minutes. Remove pan from oven, let lasagna settle for 5 minutes, and serve.

Cook's Note: Because the pesto and béchamel layers are so thin, I like to make this dish with eight layers of pasta instead of the standard six. If you're using fresh Spinach Pasta, use ⅔ package of spinach, 3¼ cups flour, and 4 eggs. For Basil and Garlic Pasta, use 2⅔ cups flour, 4 eggs, ⅔ cup basil, and 3 cloves garlic.

Lasagna with Baked Squash, Prosciutto, and Pine Nuts

Creamy hard squash is teamed with prosciutto and toasted pine nuts to make an unusual but appealing combination. Butternut squash can be used in place of acorn squash.

SERVES 6–8

2 large (about 4 pounds) acorn squash
2 tablespoons unsalted butter
½ cup milk
1 tablespoon minced fresh sage leaves
1 teaspoon salt
¼ teaspoon freshly ground white pepper
1 recipe Egg Pasta **or** ***Herb Pasta (see Index)*** **or** ***18 dried lasagna noodles***
1½ cups Béchamel Sauce (see Index)
½ pound thinly sliced prosciutto **or** ***baked ham, cut into 1-inch squares***
⅔ cup pine nuts, lightly toasted (see Cook's Note)
1½ cups freshly grated Parmesan cheese

1. Preheat oven to 400°F. Halve squash and scoop out seeds and stringy pulp. Place squash, cut side down, on a greased baking sheet and bake until flesh is tender, about 45 minutes. Remove squash from oven and cool. Do not turn off oven.

2. Scoop pulp from cooled squash and place in the work bowl of a food processor. (You should have about 4 cups pulp.) Add butter, milk, sage, salt, and pepper and puree until smooth.

3. Cook and drain pasta.

4. Grease a 13″ × 9″ lasagna pan. Smear 3 tablespoons béchamel across bottom. Line bottom with a layer of pasta, making sure noodles touch but do not overlap. Spread ¾ cup squash puree over noodles. Sprinkle with several tablespoons each of ham, pine nuts, and cheese and drizzle with 3 tablespoons béchamel. Repeat layering of pasta, squash puree, ham, pine nuts, cheese, and béchamel four more times. For the sixth layer, coat noodles with 6 tablespoons béchamel and sprinkle with remaining ½ cup cheese.

5. Bake lasagna in 400°F oven until top turns golden brown in spots, about 20 minutes. Remove pan from oven, let lasagna settle for 5 minutes, and serve.

Cook's Note: To toast nuts, place them on a baking sheet and bake in a 325°F oven for 5 minutes. Pine nuts burn quite easily, so check them often as they toast.

Spring Lasagna with Leeks and Artichokes

The combination of leeks and artichokes with fontina cheese and plenty of fresh thyme is a perfect way to greet spring.

SERVES 6–8

4 large leeks
2 tablespoons olive oil
1½ teaspoons salt
½ teaspoon freshly ground black pepper
1 tablespoon minced fresh thyme leaves
4 large artichokes, trimmed (see page 93)
3 cloves garlic, minced
1 tablespoon fresh lemon juice
½ cup dry white wine
¼ cup minced fresh parsley leaves
1 recipe Egg Pasta* or *Herb Pasta (see Index)* or *18 dried lasagna noodles
1½ cups Béchamel Sauce (see Index)
¾ pound fontina cheese, shredded
¾ cup freshly grated Parmesan cheese

1. Trim and discard dark green part of leeks. Slice remaining white and light green part in half and carefully separate layers under cold running water to remove dirt. If leeks are particularly dirty, place in a large bowl and rinse in several changes of cold water. Thinly slice leeks and set aside.

2. Heat oil in a very large saucepan. Add leeks, ½ teaspoon of the salt, ¼ teaspoon of the pepper, and 1 teaspoon of the thyme and sauté over medium heat until wilted, about 5 minutes. Drain prepared artichokes and add to pan along with garlic, lemon juice, and wine. Cover and simmer over medium heat until artichokes are tender but not mushy, about 20 minutes.

3. Uncover saucepan, stir in parsley, remaining teaspoon salt, and remaining ¼ teaspoon black pepper and simmer until any remaining liquid evaporates. (This should take no longer than 2 minutes.) Set mixture aside.

4. Cook and drain pasta. Stir remaining 2 teaspoons thyme into prepared béchamel. Preheat oven to 400°F.

5. Grease a 13″ × 9″ lasagna pan. Smear 3 tablespoons béchamel across bottom. Line bottom with a layer of pasta, making sure noodles touch but do not overlap. Spread 1 cup artichoke and leek mixture over noodles. Drizzle with 3 tablespoons béchamel and sprinkle with ½ cup fontina and 2 tablespoons Parmesan. Repeat layering of pasta, vegetable mixture, béchamel, and two cheeses four more times. For the sixth layer, coat noodles with 6 tablespoons béchamel and sprinkle with remaining cheeses (about 1 cup fontina and 3 tablespoons Parmesan).

6. Bake lasagna until cheese turns golden brown in spots, about 20 minutes. Remove pan from oven, let lasagna settle for 5 minutes, and serve.

Lasagna with Endive and Radicchio

Gruyère cheese complements the smokiness of pancetta (Italian bacon), the sweetness of Belgian endive, and the bitterness of radicchio. This rich dish is perfect for a cold winter night.

SERVES 6–8

1 tablespoon olive oil
1 onion, chopped fine
2 cloves garlic, minced fine
⅓ pound pancetta* or *bacon, cut into ½-inch squares
1½ pounds Belgian endive, roots trimmed and leaves cut into ¼-inch-wide strips
1 pound radicchio, cored and cut into ¼-inch-wide strips
½ teaspoon freshly ground black pepper
Salt to taste
1 recipe Egg Pasta* or *Black Pepper Pasta (see Index)* or *18 dried lasagna noodles
1½ cups Béchamel Sauce (see Index)
¾ pound Gruyère cheese, shredded

1. Heat oil in a large saucepan. Add onion and sauté over medium heat until translucent, about 5 minutes. Stir in garlic and pancetta and continue cooking over medium heat for about 3 minutes, stirring occasionally so pancetta squares separate.

2. Stir in endive and coat well with oil. Sauté, stirring occasionally so cooked endive is pulled to the top of the pan, until all the endive is wilted, about 7 minutes. Add radicchio and stir constantly until radicchio loses its bright red color and softens, about 2 minutes. Stir in pepper and taste for salt. (If the bacon is very salty, there may be no need to add salt.) Set mixture aside.

3. Cook and drain pasta. Preheat oven to 400°F.

4. Grease a 13″ × 9″ lasagna pan. Smear 3 tablespoons béchamel across bottom. Line bottom with a layer of pasta, making sure noodles touch but do not overlap. Spread 1 cup endive and radicchio mixture over noodles. Drizzle with 3 tablespoons béchamel and sprinkle with ½ cup cheese. Repeat layering of pasta, vegetables, béchamel, and cheese four more times. For the sixth layer, coat pasta with 6 tablespoons béchamel and sprinkle with remaining 1 cup cheese.

5. Bake lasagna until cheese turns golden brown in spots, 20 to 25 minutes. Remove pan from oven, let lasagna settle for 5 minutes, and serve.

Parsley Lasagna with Scallops and Bread Crumbs

♣

This delicately flavored dish is remarkably simple to assemble and makes an elegant statement. If you don't have time to make your own parsley noodles, buy any fresh herb noodles you can find. This is one of the few recipes where thicker dried noodles just don't deliver the same results. Since there are so few ingredients, try making your own bread crumbs from stale high-quality bread. They are vastly superior to store-bought crumbs.

SERVES 6

6 slices day-old Italian bread or ***½ cup unseasoned commercial bread crumbs***
6 tablespoons olive oil
1 tablespoon finely minced garlic
1 pound scallops, tendons removed (see Cook's Note), cut into very small dice
2 tablespoons minced fresh parsley leaves
1 teaspoon salt
1 recipe Herb Pasta (see Index) made with parsley
2 cups Béchamel Sauce (see Index)

1. Cut bread into small chunks and grind in a food processor fitted with the metal blade. Use a strainer to separate the fine crumbs from the larger chunks of bread. Measure out about 1 cup fine crumbs (they will shrink to about ½ cup when toasted) and reserve coarse crumbs in an airtight container. Heat a large skillet and toast fine crumbs over medium-low heat, stirring occasionally to prevent burning, until golden brown. Set ½ cup toasted crumbs aside and reserve any additional crumbs in the airtight container. (If you're using store-bought crumbs, simply toast until golden and set aside.)

2. Heat olive oil in a medium-size skillet. Add garlic and sauté over medium heat until pale yellow, about 2 minutes. Add scallops and raise heat to medium-high. Sauté until scallops turn opaque and are cooked through, about 4 minutes. Stir in parsley and salt and scrape mixture into a large bowl.

3. Cook and drain pasta. Stir 1½ cups prepared béchamel into bowl with reserved scallops and set remaining ½ cup béchamel aside. Preheat oven to 375°F.

4. Grease a 13″ × 9″ lasagna pan. Smear 3 tablespoons of the reserved béchamel across bottom. Line bottom with a layer of pasta, making sure noodles touch but do not overlap. Spread a generous ½ cup of the scallops and sauce over noodles. Make sure sauce fully coats noodles while scallops dot the surface. Sprinkle with 1 tablespoon bread crumbs. Repeat layering of pasta, scallop mixture, and bread crumbs four more times. For the sixth layer, coat noodles with remaining 5 tablespoons béchamel and sprinkle with remaining 3 tablespoons bread crumbs.

5. Bake lasagna until top turns golden and sauce is bubbling, about 15 minutes. Remove pan from oven, let lasagna settle for 5 minutes, and serve.

Cook's Note: Some scallops come with a small tendon attached to the side of the meat. The tendon can be tough when cooked and should be peeled away and discarded.

Lasagna with Shrimp and Sun-Dried Tomato Sauce

Sun-dried tomatoes add a wonderful flavor and color to béchamel sauce. This elegant combination is best with Herb Pasta or Basil and Garlic Pasta.

SERVES 6

3 ounces sun-dried tomatoes (not packed in oil)
2 tablespoons unsalted butter
1 pound shrimp, shelled, deveined, and minced
Salt and freshly ground pepper to taste
3 cloves garlic
⅓ cup olive oil
1 recipe Herb Pasta **or** ***Basil and Garlic Pasta (see Index)*** **or** ***18 dried lasagna noodles***
2 cups Béchamel Sauce (see Index)
1¼ cups freshly grated Parmesan cheese

1. Place sun-dried tomatoes in a small bowl and cover with several cups boiling water. Soak for about 30 minutes.

2. Meanwhile, heat butter in a medium-size skillet. Add shrimp and sauté over medium heat, stirring occasionally, until cooked through, about 3 minutes. Season with salt and pepper and set aside in a large bowl.

3. Drain tomatoes and reserve ¼ cup soaking liquid. Puree garlic in a food processor. Add tomatoes and reserved soaking liquid and puree until smooth. With machine running, add olive oil in a steady stream through feed tube. Scrape sun-dried tomato sauce into a bowl and season with salt and pepper to taste.

4. Cook and drain pasta. Combine prepared béchamel with sun-dried tomato sauce. Reserve ½ cup sun-dried tomato béchamel and mix the rest into bowl with shrimp. Check shrimp mixture for salt and pepper. Preheat oven to 400°F.

5. Grease a 13″ × 9″ lasagna pan. Smear ¼ cup of the reserved sun-dried tomato béchamel across bottom. Line bottom with a layer of pasta, making sure noodles touch but do not overlap. Smear ⅔ cup shrimp mixture over pasta, making sure sauce coats noodles well. Sprinkle with 3 tablespoons cheese. Repeat layering of pasta, shrimp sauce, and cheese four more times. For the sixth layer, coat pasta with remaining ¼ cup sun-dried tomato béchamel and sprinkle with remaining 5 tablespoons cheese.

6. Bake lasagna until top turns golden brown in spots and sauce is bubbling, 15 to 20 minutes. Remove pan from oven, let lasagna settle for 5 minutes, and serve.

Cook's Note: Although I prefer rehydrating sun-dried tomatoes myself, tomatoes packed in oil can be used. Simply skip the soaking step and puree drained tomatoes with several extra tablespoons of oil.

Black Pepper Lasagna with Caramelized Onions and Pancetta

This recipe demonstrates the principle that a few perfectly matched ingredients can indeed create a dish with depth of flavor. Slow-cooking onions until they are very soft releases their sweetness and makes them an excellent accompaniment to salty pancetta. Pancetta, an unsmoked Italian bacon, is available at better supermarkets and Italian delis. American bacon may be used instead.

SERVES 6

1 tablespoon olive oil
½ pound pancetta** or **bacon, cut into ½-inch squares
4 large (about 2 pounds) onions
1½ cups Béchamel Sauce (see Index)
Salt to taste
1 recipe Black Pepper Pasta** or **Egg Pasta (see Index)** or **18 dried lasagna noodles
1 cup freshly grated Parmesan cheese

1. Heat oil in a large nonstick skillet. Add pancetta and fry over medium heat until crisp, about 10 minutes. Use a slotted spoon to transfer pancetta to a large bowl.

2. Meanwhile, remove and discard thick outer layer from each onion. Slice onions into thin rings. Add onions to the empty skillet and cook in bacon fat, stirring occasionally, until they have softened completely and are light brown in color, about 30 minutes. If onions start to stick, add more oil and reduce heat. When finished, the onions should be very soft but not too deeply colored.

3. Scrape cooked onions into bowl with pancetta. Add 1 cup prepared béchamel to bowl with onions. Mix well and taste for salt. (If the pancetta is salty,

it may not need any.) Set onion mixture and remaining ½ cup béchamel sauce aside separately.

4. Cook and drain pasta. Preheat oven to 400°F.

5. Grease a 13″ × 9″ lasagna pan. Smear 3 tablespoons reserved béchamel across bottom. Line bottom with a layer of pasta, making sure noodles touch but do not overlap. Spread ½ cup onion mixture over noodles, making sure béchamel in the mixture coats all parts of the pasta. Sprinkle with 2 tablespoons cheese. Repeat layering of pasta, onions, and cheese four more times. For the sixth layer, coat pasta with remaining 5 tablespoons béchamel and sprinkle with remaining 6 tablespoons cheese.

6. Bake lasagna until top turns golden in spots and sauce is bubbling, 15 to 20 minutes. Remove pan from oven, let lasagna settle for 5 minutes, and serve.

Cook's Note: If you're using plain noodles, add ½ teaspoon freshly ground black pepper to the onion and béchamel mixture.

Chicken Liver Lasagna with Balsamic Vinegar and Tomatoes

This rich, earthy lasagna is Tuscan in spirit. Chicken livers are sautéed with balsamic vinegar and then enriched with tomatoes and stock. This hearty dish is quite rich and needs only a simple salad as an accompaniment.

SERVES 6–8

3 tablespoons olive oil
¼ cup finely minced shallot
¼ cup finely minced carrot
1 pound chicken livers, trimmed of fat and chopped into very small pieces
⅛ teaspoon freshly grated nutmeg
1 teaspoon salt
½ teaspoon freshly ground black pepper
3 tablespoons balsamic vinegar
½ cup chicken stock
2 cups canned crushed tomatoes
¼ cup chopped fresh parsley leaves
1 recipe Egg Pasta or Spinach Pasta (see Index) or 18 dried lasagna noodles
1½ cups Béchamel Sauce (see Index)
1 cup freshly grated Parmesan Cheese

1. Heat oil in a large saucepan. Add shallot and carrot and sauté over medium heat until softened but not colored, about 5 minutes.

2. Add livers, nutmeg, salt, and pepper and cook, stirring frequently, until liver is light brown on the outside, about 2 minutes. Add vinegar and simmer until

it evaporates and liver is cooked through, another 2 minutes or so. Add chicken stock and simmer for 3 minutes. Add tomatoes and simmer gently until sauce thickens, about 20 minutes. Stir in parsley and taste for salt. Set aside.

3. Cook and drain pasta. Preheat oven to 400°F.

4. Grease a 13″ × 9″ lasagna pan. Smear ¼ cup béchamel across bottom. Line bottom with a layer of pasta, making sure noodles touch but do not overlap. Spread ⅔ cup chicken liver sauce over noodles. Drizzle with 3 tablespoons béchamel and sprinkle with 2 tablespoons cheese. Repeat layering of pasta, chicken liver sauce, béchamel, and cheese four more times. For the sixth layer, coat noodles with remaining 5 tablespoons béchamel and sprinkle with remaining 6 tablespoons cheese.

5. Bake lasagna until top turns golden brown in spots and sauce is bubbling, about 20 minutes. Remove pan from oven, let lasagna settle for 5 minutes, and serve.

-7-

Loosely Lasagna

Louisiana Lasagna
Greek Lasagna
Mexican Polenta Lasagna with Shrimp and Ancho Chilies
Tortilla Lasagna with Chicken, Corn, and Fresh Tomato Salsa
Tiramisù
Italian Bread Pudding with Apples and Rummy Raisins
Zuppa Inglese

Louisiana Lasagna

Shrimp and andouille (a spicy pork sausage often used in New Orleans kitchens) ignite a fiery tomato sauce. Parmesan cheese and rich béchamel round out the flavors in this American-inspired lasagna.

SERVES 6–8

2 tablespoons olive oil
½ pound andouille sausage
½ pound medium-size shrimp, peeled, deveined, and each cut into 3 or 4 pieces
1 tablespoon finely minced garlic
3 scallions, white and light green parts only, sliced into thin rings
1 teaspoon minced fresh oregano leaves or ½ teaspoon dried
1 teaspoon paprika
¼ teaspoon Tabasco or other hot sauce
½ teaspoon salt
3 cups canned crushed tomatoes
1 recipe Egg Pasta **or** ***Black Pepper Pasta (see Index)*** **or** ***18 dried lasagna noodles***
1¾ cups Béchamel Sauce (see Index)
1 cup freshly grated Parmesan cheese

1. Heat oil in a medium-size saucepan. Squeeze sausage from casings directly into pan. Cook over medium heat until sausage is nicely browned, about 5 minutes. Stir in shrimp, garlic, scallions, oregano, paprika, Tabasco, and salt. Sauté, stirring often, until the shrimp turn bright pink, about 3 minutes.

2. Add tomatoes and simmer until sauce thickens slightly, about 15 minutes. Taste for salt and set aside.

3. Cook and drain pasta. Preheat oven to 400°F.

4. Grease a 13″ × 9″ lasagna pan. Smear 3 tablespoons béchamel across bottom. Line bottom with a layer of pasta, making sure noodles touch but do not overlap. Cover pasta with ⅔ cup tomato sauce. Drizzle with ¼ cup béchamel and sprinkle with 2 tablespoons cheese. Repeat layering of pasta, tomato sauce, béchamel, and cheese four more times. For the sixth layer, coat pasta with 5 tablespoons béchamel and sprinkle with remaining 6 tablespoons cheese.

5. Bake lasagna until top turns golden brown in spots and sauce is bubbling, about 20 minutes. Remove pan from oven, let lasagna settle for 5 minutes, and serve.

Cook's Note: Other spicy pork sausages may be substituted for the andouille.

Greek Lasagna

This dish takes its cues from pastitsio, a baked ziti dish redolent of cinnamon and nutmeg. In this version I have used the basic meat sauce from the Greek classic to make a layered lasagna. The results are wonderful.

SERVES 8

2 tablespoons olive oil
1 onion, chopped fine
1 carrot, chopped fine
1 pound ground beef
1 teaspoon ground cinnamon plus a dash for béchamel
½ teaspoon freshly grated nutmeg plus a dash for béchamel
1½ teaspoons salt
¼ cup dry white wine
2 cups canned crushed tomatoes
1½ cups Béchamel Sauce (see Index)
1 recipe Egg Pasta* or *Spinach Pasta (see Index)* or *18 dried lasagna noodles
1 cup freshly grated Parmesan cheese

1. Heat oil in a large saucepan. Add the onion and sauté over medium heat until translucent, about 5 minutes. Add carrot and cook until slightly softened, about 5 minutes. Stir in ground beef and crumble with a fork. Continue cooking until the meat loses its red color, about 4 minutes.

2. Stir in cinnamon, nutmeg, salt, wine, and tomatoes. Bring mixture to a boil, reduce heat to low, and simmer gently until sauce thickens, about 30 minutes. Taste for salt and set aside.

3. Stir a dash of cinnamon and nutmeg into prepared béchamel. Set sauce aside.

4. Cook and drain pasta. Preheat oven to 400°F.

5. Grease a 13″ × 9″ lasagna pan. Smear 3 tablespoons béchamel across bottom. Line bottom with a layer of pasta, making sure noodles touch but do not overlap. Spread ¾ cup meat sauce over noodles. Drizzle with 3 tablespoons béchamel sauce and sprinkle with 2 tablespoons cheese. Repeat layering of pasta, meat sauce, béchamel, and cheese four more times. For the sixth layer, coat noodles with 6 tablespoons béchamel and sprinkle with remaining 6 tablespoons cheese.

6. Bake lasagna until top turns golden brown in spots and sauce is bubbling, about 20 minutes. Remove pan from oven, let lasagna settle for 5 minutes, and serve.

Cook's Note: If desired, the meat sauce can be made with half ground lamb and half ground beef.

Mexican Polenta Lasagna with Shrimp and Ancho Chilies

♣

Dried chilies are a wonderful addition to tomato sauces. This recipe calls for relatively mild anchos, the name given to poblano peppers that have been dried. Other dried chilies such as mulatos or pasillas may be used, but make adjustments for heat. Soaking chilies releases their flavor, and the liquid is also added to the sauce.

SERVES 8

6 ancho chilies
2 cups hot water
2 tablespoons olive oil
6 cloves garlic, minced
4 cups canned crushed tomatoes
1 teaspoon salt or to taste
1 pound medium-size shrimp, peeled and deveined
3 tablespoons minced fresh cilantro leaves
1 recipe Polenta (see Index)
1 pound queso fresco* or *Monterey Jack cheese, shredded

1. Wash chilies under warm running water (use rubber gloves while handling). Place chilies in a small bowl and cover with hot water. Soak for 20 minutes. Drain chilies and reserve liquid. Make a slit on the side of each chile and scrape out the seeds and any fleshy white veins. If necessary, rinse chilies under running water to remove all the seeds. Remove and discard chili stems. Place cleaned chilies and soaking liquid in a food processor or blender and puree until smooth. Set aside.

2. Heat oil in a large saucepan. Add garlic and sauté over medium heat until golden, about 1 minute. Add tomatoes, chile puree, and salt. Simmer gently until

sauce thickens slightly, about 20 minutes. Add shrimp and cilantro and cook just until shrimp are pink, about 3 minutes. Do not overcook shrimp. Add more salt if needed and set sauce aside.

3. Pour half of prepared polenta into a greased 13″ × 9″ lasagna pan and the other half onto a greased 13″ × 9″ baking sheet. Cool polenta for about 10 minutes. Meanwhile, preheat oven to 400°F.

4. Spread half of the shrimp sauce over polenta in lasagna pan and sprinkle with half the cheese. Cut polenta on baking sheet into four pieces and transfer pieces one at a time to the lasagna pan, making sure the first layer is completely covered. Spread remaining shrimp sauce over second layer of polenta and sprinkle with remaining cheese.

5. Cover pan with aluminum foil and bake lasagna for 15 minutes. Remove foil and continue baking until cheese turns golden brown in spots and sauce is bubbling, about 5 minutes more. Remove pan from oven, let lasagna settle for 10 minutes, and serve.

Cook's Note: Unlike lasagna made with pasta, this dish cannot be assembled ahead of time. However, the shrimp sauce and polenta can be prepared separately. Refrigerate sauce in an airtight container and reheat before using. Wrap the polenta tightly with plastic and refrigerate overnight. Let the polenta come to room temperature before assembling the dish.

Tortilla Lasagna with Chicken, Corn, and Fresh Tomato Salsa

For this Mexican-inspired "lasagna," flour tortillas are layered with spicy strips of sautéed chicken, corn kernels, and a cilantro-spiked tomato salsa. The lasagna is baked in a large soufflé dish and served in wedges.

SERVES 6

1¼ pounds plum tomatoes, diced small
2 scallions, white and light green parts only, sliced into thin rings
1 tablespoon chopped fresh cilantro leaves
3 cloves garlic, minced
1½ teaspoons salt
Tabasco or other hot sauce **or** ***minced jalapeño chilies to taste***
2 tablespoons olive oil
1 pound skinless, boneless chicken breasts
1 teaspoon chili powder
½ teaspoon ground cumin
1 9-ounce package frozen corn kernels, thawed
5 9-inch flour tortillas
¾ pound Monterey Jack cheese, shredded

1. Toss tomatoes, scallions, cilantro, garlic, 1 teaspoon of the salt, and hot sauce in a bowl. Set this salsa aside.

2. Heat oil in a large skillet. Trim fat from chicken breasts and cut crosswise into ¼-inch strips. Add chicken, spices, and remaining ½ teaspoon salt to pan and sauté, stirring often, until chicken is cooked through, about 5 minutes.

3. Add corn and continue cooking until corn is hot and any liquid in the pan has evaporated, about 3 minutes more. Taste for salt and set aside.

4. Preheat oven to 400°F. Grease a 9-inch round soufflé dish or casserole that is 3 inches deep. Lay one tortilla on bottom. Spread ¾ cup chicken and corn mixture over tortilla and cover with ½ cup salsa and ½ cup cheese. (Use a slotted spoon to transfer both chicken and salsa to measuring cups to make sure you leave any liquid behind.) Repeat layering of tortillas, chicken, salsa, and cheese three more times. For the fifth layer, cover tortilla with remaining ½ cup salsa and sprinkle with remaining 1 cup cheese.

5. Bake lasagna until cheese turns golden brown in spots, about 25 minutes. Remove dish from oven, let lasagna settle for 10 minutes, cut into wedges, and serve.

Tiramisù

This classic Italian dessert is made with two layers of espresso-soaked cookies and a rich mascarpone filling dusted with bittersweet chocolate. The name translates as "pick me up," an apt description for this easy-to-prepare sweet that is often served as a midafternoon snack in Italy.

SERVES 10

6 large eggs at room temperature, separated
3 tablespoons sugar
1 pound mascarpone cheese (see Cook's Note)
2 tablespoons brandy* or *coffee-flavored liqueur
1 teaspoon vanilla extract
1½ cups brewed espresso* or *very strong coffee, cooled
30 Italian ladyfingers (see Cook's Note)
½ pound bittersweet chocolate, chopped into very small pieces by hand or pulsed briefly in a food processor

1. Beat egg yolks and sugar in an electric mixer until light yellow in color, about 1 minute. Add mascarpone, brandy, and vanilla and mix well. Beat egg whites in a separate bowl until stiff but not dry. Gently fold whites into mascarpone mixture and set aside briefly.

2. Pour cooled espresso into a wide, shallow bowl. Dip ladyfingers into coffee one a time and arrange in a 13″ × 9″ lasagna pan. Use half of the cookies to cover bottom of pan.

3. Spread half of the mascarpone mixture over cookies and then sprinkle with half of the chocolate.

4. Dip remaining cookies in espresso and make a second layer of cookies on top of the chocolate. Spread remaining mascarpone mixture over second layer of cookies and sprinkle with remaining chocolate.

5. Cover pan tightly with plastic wrap and refrigerate for 4 hours. (This allows time for the cookies and filling to blend.) Tiramisù may be refrigerated for up to 8 hours. Serve chilled.

Cook's Note: Mascarpone is an Italian cream cheese that is much creamier and a bit sweeter than commercial American products. Although commercial American cream cheeses—most made with gums and stabilizers—should not be used in this recipe, fresh cream cheese may be used if you can find it. However, with the boom in authentic Italian food products, it's probably easier to find fresh mascarpone in better supermarkets, gourmet stores, or Italian delicatessens.

Italian ladyfingers are long, crisp cookies with oval edges. Look for them at gourmet stores or Italian markets. They are sometimes called *savioardi.*

Italian Bread Pudding with Apples and Rummy Raisins

❦

Bread pudding, a rich custard thickened with slices of bread, is one of my favorite desserts. In this version caramelized apples and rum-soaked raisins are sandwiched between layers of Italian bread that are then covered with a cinnamon-flavored custard. This layered dessert is homey but also quite impressive.

SERVES 8–10

½ cup raisins
3 tablespoons rum
4 large eggs
1 cup granulated sugar
1 quart half-and-half
1 teaspoon ground cinnamon
1½ teaspoons vanilla extract
2 tablespoons unsalted butter
3 large (about 1¼ pounds) tart apples, peeled, cored, quartered, and sliced thin
1 loaf (about ¾ pound), stale Italian bread, cut into ½-inch-thick slices
1 tablespoon confectioners' sugar

1. Preheat oven to 350°F and butter a 13″ × 9″ lasagna pan. You also need a large roasting pan that will comfortably hold the lasagna pan.

2. Place raisins and rum in a small bowl and soak, stirring occasionally, for about 30 minutes.

3. Beat eggs and ¾ cup of the granulated sugar until pale yellow in color, about 1 minute. Whisk in half-and-half, cinnamon, and vanilla and set aside when well mixed.

4. Melt butter in a large skillet. Add apple slices and cook until slightly softened, about 4 minutes. Stir in raisins and rum and simmer for about 2 minutes to cook off some of the alcohol. Sprinkle remaining ¼ cup granulated sugar over apples and toss occasionally until liquid in pan thickens a bit and apples start to caramelize, about 4 minutes.

5. Line bottom of lasagna pan with a layer of bread. Spread apple mixture evenly over bread and cover with a second layer of bread. Pour cinnamon custard over bread and press down so that the bread absorbs as much custard as possible. Set lasagna pan aside for 10 minutes and press down on bread occasionally.

6. Transfer lasagna pan to a larger, deeper roasting pan. Place roasting pan in the center of a preheated oven. Carefully pour boiling water into outside roasting pan and fill about halfway up the sides of the lasagna pan. Close oven door and bake until pudding puffs and knife inserted into the center comes out clean, about 45 minutes. Remove lasagna pan from oven and let bread pudding cool for 30 minutes. (Bread pudding can be cooled completely and served at room temperature if desired.)

7. Sift confectioners' sugar over pudding and serve warm with vanilla ice cream or whipped cream if desired.

Cook's Note: Many custard-based desserts are cooked in a water bath to ensure a smooth texture. In this recipe the lasagna pan is placed in a large roasting pan that is then partially filled with boiling water. The water keeps the oven heat from curdling the custard.

Stale bread will absorb more custard and therefore works best in most bread pudding recipes, including this one. If you have only fresh bread, place slices in a 200°F oven for 15 minutes to dry them out.

Zuppa Inglese

✤

Zuppa Inglese, or "English soup," is a triflelike dessert served in trattorias throughout Italy. Thin slices of buttery pound cake are soaked in rum and raspberry liqueur and then layered with rich pastry cream. The pudding must be refrigerated for several hours before serving to allow the flavors to blend and the cake to soften adequately.

SERVES 6–8

1 small (about 12 ounces) pound cake
3 tablespoons rum
⅓ cup raspberry liqueur
2½ cups milk
4 large egg yolks
⅔ cup sugar
3 tablespoons cornstarch
1 teaspoon vanilla extract
⅓ cup seedless raspberry jam

1. Cut pound cake into ¼-inch-thick slices. Cut slices in half and set aside.

2. Combine rum and raspberry liqueur in a small bowl and set aside.

3. Heat milk in a medium-size saucepan. Don't let milk come to a boil.

4. Meanwhile, whisk yolks and sugar in a bowl until pale yellow and creamy, about 1 minute. Whisk in cornstarch and mix well.

5. Slowly whisk ½ cup hot milk from saucepan into yolk mixture. When combined, pour yolk mixture into saucepan and whisk constantly over medium-low heat until pastry cream thickens. (This will take several minutes.) Remove custard from heat just before it comes to a boil and stir in vanilla extract.

6. Smear bottom and sides of a sloped 2-quart bowl with ¼ cup hot pastry cream. Line bottom and sides of bowl with a layer of pound cake slices. Do not

overlap slices. Use a pastry brush to soak cake with liqueur mixture. Spread ¾ cup pastry cream over soaked cake slices. Make another layer of cake slices and brush to soak in more liqueur. Cover with another ¾ cup pastry cream. Make a third layer of cake slices and brush with remaining liqueur mixture. Spread raspberry jam over cake slices and cover with remaining pastry cream.

7. Wrap bowl tightly in plastic and refrigerate for at least 2 hours for flavors to blend and cake to soften. Zuppa Inglese may be refrigerated overnight. Scoop portions into serving bowls and dollop with whipped cream if desired.

Cook's Note: If you plan on serving the dessert at the table, use a glass bowl so that the alternating layers of cake and custard are visible.

INDEX